EX·LIBRIS
Rev. George N. Vida
10

# Art Treasures of the Vatican Library

Leonard von Matt

# ART TREASURES OF THE VATICAN LIBRARY

Text by
Georg Daltrop and Adriano Prandi

Harry N. Abrams, Inc., Publishers, New York

Translated by Robert Allen

Standard Book Number: 8109–0528–0
Library of Congress Catalogue Card Number: 74–125782


Harry N. Abrams, Incorporated, New York

Printed and bound in West Germany

TO THE MEMORY OF
THE REVEREND PAULUS KUENZLE

Musaeorum Bibliothecae Vaticanae Curator
February 8, 1906 (Saint Gall)–June 20, 1968 (Rome)

# Contents

# The Art Collections of the Biblioteca Apostolica Vaticana

## Historical Introduction

From the north side of the cupola of Saint Peter's in Rome, one can look down on the whole complex of buildings—the Vatican museums, library, and archives—that surround the Belvedere Courtyard and divide it into three terraces lying at different levels (plate 1; in the photograph, the terraces ascend from right to left). Pope Julius II (1503–13) wanted to link the Papal Palace with the summer villa that Innocent VIII (1484–92) had erected on the Vatican hill. According to the sixteenth-century art historian Giorgio Vasari, Julius' first idea was to enclose the little hollow between the villa and the palace to form a rectangular theater, with access through arches to a gallery on either side. Bramante drew the plans and started work on what Vasari said was such a splendid project that nothing finer had been seen in Rome since ancient times. But the pope died, and his architect too soon after, with the result that the building was left unfinished.

Under Pius IV (1559–65) the façade with the "Nicchione" that forms the north end (upper left in plate 1) was completed in accordance with a new design by Pirro Ligorio. Sixtus V (1585–90) had Domenico Fontana build a new library wing across the courtyard at the point where the lower and middle terraces were connected by a row of steps. Pius VII (1800–1823) commissioned Raphael Stern to erect the "Braccio Nuovo" of the Sculpture Museum where the middle and upper terraces met. The art collections of the Vatican Library are displayed on what is the ground floor at the north end and becomes the second floor at the south end of the gallery 1,426 feet long forming the west side of the complex (to the left in plate 1).

After the popes returned from Avignon in 1377, the papal library became famous under Nicholas (1447–55). But it is not until almost a century later that the first mention appears of a sort of art collection, more probably a cabinet of curios, there. At that time the prefect of the library was Marcello Cervini, who was elected to the Holy See as Marcellus II in 1555 but wore the tiara for only twenty days. On February 21, 1600, Fulvio Orsini bequeathed to

◁ 1 View from the Dome of Saint Peter's over the Belvedere Courtyard and Vatican Museums and Library

Clement VIII in his will four coins of Constantine I, the first Roman emperor to convert to Christianity, and his son Crispus. The legacy is interesting more for its motivation than for its value: Orsini's intention was not merely to enrich the library with ancient coins but also to present it with relics recalling an event of first importance in the history of the Church, in order that they might be viewed by all and sundry *(ut omnibus in promptu sint ecclesiasticae antiquitatis curiosis)*.

In 1756, by order of Benedict XIV, Christian antiquities and documents from the Church's earliest times were displayed at the southern end of the long gallery that closes the Belvedere Courtyard on the west. This was the origin of the Museo Sacro. Its foundation is still recorded in an inscription over the entrance: "To enhance the City's magnificence and demonstrate the truth of Religion by means of Christianity's sacred monuments" *(Ad augendum Urbis splendorem et asserendum Religionis veritatem sacris Christianorum monumentis)*. For the purpose, the pope brought together a number of private collections, of which Cardinal Gaspare Carpegna's was probably the most important. As Vicar of Rome from 1671 to 1714, the cardinal had collected antiquities found in the catacombs. On the advice of the papal librarian, Cardinal Passionei, Benedict XIV purchased the collection from Carpegna's heirs in 1741. Of his own property the pope added the gifts he had received. These included the Chigi collection and the beautiful gold glasses that had belonged to the Florentine senator Filippo Buonarroti and had been stored in the Quirinal Palace for the last seventeen years. Also placing his collection of antiquities at the pope's disposal was Francesco Vettori; on September 30, 1757, he was appointed the first curator *(Musaeorum Bibliothecae Vaticanae Curator)* of the newly arranged collection for life.

On August 4, 1761, Clement XIII issued a brief ordering that the secular portion of the Carpegna collection should be stored in the north wing of the long west gallery of the Belvedere Courtyard. There the Museo Profano was set up in 1767, at the suggestion and instigation of the papal librarian, Cardinal Alessandro Albani, to preserve the Roman antiquities *(servandis Romanae antiquitatis monumentis)*, as the inscription over the doorway says. Cardinal Albani's adviser, Johann Joachim Winckelmann, had already been appointed commissioner of all antiquities in and around Rome on April 9, 1763. But the Museo Profano was not completely installed until the pontificate of Pius VI (1775–99). It is a typical example of the combined museum and numismatic collection so greatly favored at the end of the eighteenth century. The cabinets were made of precious Brazilian wood that had originally been intended for the sacristy of Saint Peter's. They were designed by Luigi Daladier with the assistance of his son Giuseppe, the architect who later made his name by rearranging the layout of the Piazza del Popolo. A few years later both the numismatic collection and the antique cameos and splendid medallions from the Albani collection were carried off to Paris during the French occupation of the Holy City. In 1815 Pius VII endeavored to have them returned to Rome, but his efforts were only partly successful. Today the numismatic collection is a separate institution affiliated with the library and housed on the opposite—namely, east—side of the Belvedere Courtyard. The Museo Profano has preserved its original appearance and combines the remainders of the old collections with objects discovered in Rome between 1808 and 1815 and gifts received from the popes.

The Museo Sacro developed slowly. Successive acquisitions and transformations have given it the appearance it has today. It was opened in 1768, when Stefano Pozzi finished painting the *Triumph of the Church* and the *Three Theological Virtues* on the ceiling. In 1771 Clement XIV set up the adjoining Gabinetto dei Papiri, where the famous Ravenna Papyri dating from the sixth to the ninth century were formerly on view. Raphael Mengs painted the ceiling of the Gabinetto with the assistance of Christoph Unterberger. The allegorical composition shows History writing on the back of vanquished Time, while Fama, blowing a trumpet, points to Clement XIV's museum. The third room, the Sala degli Indirizzi, which was completed in 1818, has a ceiling decorated with the armorial bearings of Pius VII, the pope then reigning. The cabinets, which have since been altered, were originally designed by Raphael Stern. They first held Cardinal Zelada's library, then the icons of the Eastern Church; under Pius XI they were used for the addresses of homage *(indirizzi)* to Leo XIII (1878–1903) and Pius X (1903–14). Today, after systematic rearrangement, they accommodate early Christian works of art in ivory, enamel, and precious metals.

In 1838 Gregory XVI had the *Aldobrandini Wedding* (plates 8–14) transferred to an annex of this room, which is now called the Sala delle Nozze Aldobrandini from the title of that splendid work. In 1853 the fresco known as the *Vatican Odyssey* (plates 15–21), which Pius IX had received as a gift, was also placed on exhibition there. The same pope, who had set up the Commission for Christian Archaeology in 1852, ordered that all objects found in the catacombs which could not be kept on the site of their discovery should be handed over to the Museo Sacro. This led to the formation of one of the richest and most important collections of early Christian art.

During the twentieth century this museum was enormously enriched by the Treasure of the Sancta Sanctorum. In 1903 Leo XIII gave Fathers Jubaru and Grisar permission to open the shrine under the altar in the Chapel of Saint Lawrence on the Scala Santa, the pope's private oratory in the old Lateran Palace. They discovered splendid reliquaries whose contents were wrapped in precious fabrics. In 1907 Pius X ordered that the relics should be left where they were found and the containers transferred to the Vatican Library.

In 1934 Pius XI had the Treasure of the Museo Sacro rearranged. As a result, previously unknown works from the sacristy of the Sistine Chapel and other parts of the Vatican were put on view. To provide room for them, the beautiful Chapel of Pius V (1566–72) and other rooms were incorporated in the Museo Sacro at the south end of the long west wing of the Belvedere Courtyard.

The monumental splendor of their surroundings often deprives these works of art of the consideration they deserve, but for those who know how to use their eyes they open up a new world. The last *Musaeorum Bibliothecae Vaticanae Curator* devoted every effort to the worthwhile task of rousing interest in these small yet magnificent works by arranging them in a clear, functional manner. It is to him that this book owes its existence.

*G.D.*

# 1 Antique Sculpture

The antique sculpture in the Vatican Library's Museo Profano may be divided into two groups. The first serves the practical purpose of embellishing the architectural setting and consists either of columns topped with reliefs taken from earlier edifices (plates 4, 5) or of portrait heads and statues adapted to fit their new site (plates 3, 6, 7). The second group includes personal gifts presented to the Popes, such as the objects excavated at Pompeii in 1849 in the presence of Pius IX. Various tales are told about this event. Wishing to show that His Holiness had a lucky touch, one version goes, the director of the excavations at Pompeii arranged that diverse objects from the storerooms of the Naples museum be interred at a well-chosen spot on the dig, where the pope duly "discovered" them. In all probability one of the objects then unearthed was a marble votive relief showing a horse and rider (plate 2). It dates from about 400 B.C., during the classical period of ancient Greece. The Naples museum had recently received some antique sculptures from Tyndaris in Sicily, so there are good grounds for assuming that the horseman relief came from there. That, in fact, is what the keepers of the museum and other parties to the hoax said at the time. It means that the sculpture originated in a city of Sicily, which during the centuries preceding the Christian era was part of Magna Graecia and maintained close links with the mother country.

The relief shows a young horseman, whip in hand, breaking in his prancing steed. The work owes its charm to the dynamic contrast, informing every detail, between the beast's brute strength and the man's firm will. The muscular action of the two bodies—the human and the animal—is clearly limned: their rhythmic movements obey the laws of nature. The artist has captured the pair at the very moment when the rider controls his mount. In the linear structure, violent movement produces an image of calm restraint. The concept of man embodied in this work is self-explanatory and self-sufficient—in a word, classical as Hegel understood the term.

The Greek sculptor breathed life into his inanimate marble. How natural the horseman looks, how confidently he sits his steed! How free and unconstrained the motion! The whole composition is perfectly suited to the conventional space of the relief. One has the impression that law and liberty are one—a brilliant formula for disciplined living. The work mirrors a world that was capable of visualizing the idea of humanity in the image of a human being. This moment of realization of the individual's absolute uniqueness was clearly recorded in the annals of the classical age when the Greek historian Thucydides (who died about 400 B.C.) made the great statesman Pericles say in his famous funeral oration for the war dead delivered in the winter of 431–430: "We serve as examples to others" *(History of the Peloponnesian War*, II, 37). Then, for a few decades, the Greek way of life was conditioned by the harmony of an all-embracing destiny which found its perfect expression in sculpture.

The Romans were sensitive to the exemplary quality of Greek sculpture, which they collected, imitated, and copied after conquering both Magna Graecia and mainland Greece. While Augustus was emperor (27 B.C.–A.D. 14), Roman artistic production conformed to the classical Greek model. The Museo Profano offers a splendid specimen of the Augustan classicistic style in the portrait head of the emperor illustrated in plate 3.

This bronze belonged in all probability to a statue, for the ancients held that a portrait should include the entire figure. The bust as an art form was not invented until a later period of the Roman empire. We know how Augustus wanted himself to be portrayed from coins that bear his likeness and from statues that are identified by their inscriptions. This makes it an easy matter to recognize the emperor in such characteristic features as the mouth, eyes, and eyebrows and in the locks of hair combed over the forehead and temples.

The cameo of which a fragment is reproduced in plate 29 was a portrait of the same emperor. This is how Augustus is described by Suetonius, who was Hadrian's private secretary from about A.D. 119 to 121 and wrote biographies of the first twelve Caesars: "He was more than normally attractive and handsome and remained so all his life though he scorned cosmetics of any sort. . . . Both when he spoke and when he kept silent his expression was so tranquil and serene that one of the noblest Gauls confessed to his people that he was so mollified by it that he could not carry out his intention of hurling him over a precipice while crossing the Alps after gaining admission to his presence with the pretext of an interview. He had bright, shining eyes. . . . His hair curled a little" *(Lives of the Caesars*, Augustus 79).

The two porphyry columns adorned with high reliefs (plates 4 and 5) are typical examples of palace art of the late antique period. Porphyry is a very hard, dark-red stone that, as far as its color is concerned, bears a certain resemblance to purple, which was reserved for the emperor's exclusive use. The imperial substance of which these figures are made therefore warrants our viewing them as representations of the four men who jointly ruled the Roman empire at the turn of the fourth century of our era. These emperors were called Tetrarchs and governed in accordance with a system introduced by Diocletian. In A.D. 286 he chose Maximian as co-ruler, sharing with him the title Augustus, and in 293 he appointed two sub-emperors or Caesari, Galerius and Constantius Chlorus. Thus the administration of the empire was divided into four parts. On the two columns the four men are shown joined in brotherly embrace. They are dressed in the same way and carry the same attributes: a military cloak *(paludamentum)* worn over a breastplate, on the head a laurel wreath with a jewel in the center, in the left hand the globe. The work celebrates the fraternal harmony *(concordia)* thanks to which the Roman empire was once again restored to unity and order.

During the empire period, the ancient gods of the Roman-Italic pantheon and the Greek Olympus gradually lost their appeal. At the same time and to the same extent popular religions, based on the hope of meeting again after death and living happily ever after in Elysium, gained ground in many classes of society. Evidence of this is provided by tomb inscriptions. Secret cults imported from the East found many adepts. Chief among these new religions was Mithraism, which adored the Persian deity of fate and eternity, under the name of Aeon, Saeculum, Kronos, or Saturn, as the original fire, the god of heaven, the begetter of the gods, the beginning of all things, the lord of the universe and of the elements. As a rule, this deity was represented in the cult's chapels (Mithraea) in the shape of a human figure with lion's head and eagle's wings, its body encircled by a serpent's coils and covered with symbols of all sorts. Two of these images are preserved in the Museo Profano (plates 6, 7). One comes from a Mithraeum at Ostia and bears a votive inscription proving that it dates from A.D. 190.

The few sculptures assembled in the Museo Profano were acquired more by chance than by design. Yet each of them affords a glimpse into the way of life in ancient times. Even if we feel that these antique sculptures are isolated from their surroundings and have lost their original scope, they can help us to understand the ethic on which Christianity was built.

*G.D.*

2 *Horse and Rider*, Greek votive relief in marble ▷

3 Bronze portrait head of the emperor Augustus

4 and 5
Two porphyry columns, each with a pair of Tetrarchs in relief

6 Marble statue of a Mithraic deity

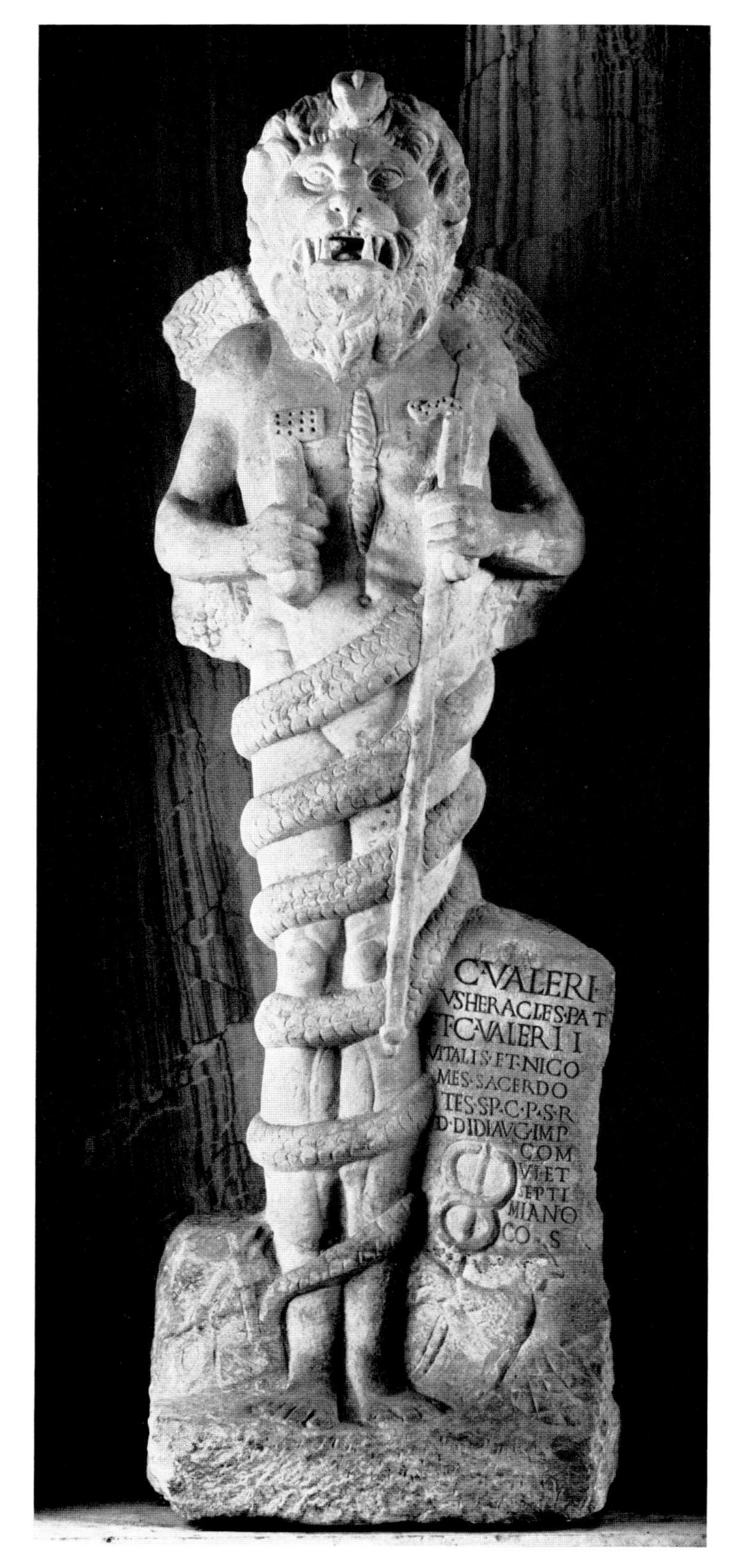


7 Marble statue of a Mithraic deity

# 2 The Aldobrandini Wedding

This friezelike mural got its high-sounding name from the theme it develops and from the man who first owned it after its discovery. He was no less important a personage than Cardinal Pietro Aldobrandini, who had received the gift of a villa from Pope Clement VIII in the year 1601. It was there that the mural, which had been discovered on the Esquiline, one of the seven hills of Rome, in 1604–5, was first set up. In 1818 Pius VII gained possession of the work, which the emperor Napoleon had endeavored in vain to secure some years before. The mural's fame had long been proclaimed in word and picture: it had been admired and studied by Rubens and Goethe, Van Dyck and Poussin, Pietro da Cortona and Andrea dal Pozzo, to name but a few. What the picture as a whole represents, namely part of a marriage ceremony, is clear to see and warrants the title it has been given. But various details nonetheless remain difficult to interpret and, owing to the fragmentary state of the work, have not yet been satisfactorily explained.

The mural is a fresco. The colors mixed with limewash were applied on the freshly plastered wall; once dry, they were firmly fixed in the plaster. Information on the technical execution of this type of mural painting is already found in ancient writings. For instance, Vitruvius, who lived during the reign of the emperor Augustus, gives a detailed description in his work on architecture (book 7, chapter 3: 5–10) of how the plaster surface is prepared and the colors laid on. And the properties of the various colors are listed in the thirty-sixth book of the *Naturalis historia* by the Elder Pliny, who lost his life in the eruption of Vesuvius in A.D. 79.

The fresco adorned an interior which was undoubtedly entirely covered with paintings, after the manner of the decorated rooms that have come down to us. This means that the *Aldobrandini Wedding* was in all likelihood part of a pictorial frieze, of which only these scenes have been preserved. The painted capital visible at the lower right beneath the "Musicians" section of the picture (plate 8) seems to indicate that the frieze was incorporated in a general scheme of mural decoration.

The picture shows ten figures rhythmically composed into three groups. The grayish violet wall that does duty as a background is divided into three sections to match the groups of figures. The two sections on the left apparently represent an interior, while the section on the right probably depicts the front of the house. The floor throughout is painted light brown.

The *Aldobrandini Wedding* can be dated to the Augustan period, at about the beginning of the Christian era. It is therefore almost contemporary with one of the greatest nuptial lyrics in Roman literature: the sixty-first poem in the collected works of Catullus

(84?–54 B.C.). In this epithalamium the poet celebrates the wedding of two noble Romans, beginning with a long hymn to Hymenaeus, the god of marriage. This is followed by a first part, which is chanted in front of the bride's house, by a second part on the way to the nuptial chamber, and by a third at the entrance to that chamber after the bride and groom have withdrawn and shut the door. With the poem in mind, one can find new meaning in the frieze.

The central group of the painting comprises two female figures seated on the edge of a couchlike bed piled with soft cushions and spread with a green coverlet (plate 10). One of the women is clothed in a white mantle that is drawn over her head and covers both her hands; this has been a bride's attire from time immemorial. Her head slightly bent, the woman seems sunk in thought. Catullus says of the bride in his wedding song:

| | |
|---|---|
| Noble shame delays: | *Tardat ingenuus pudor:* |
| . . . . . . . . . . . | . . . . . . . . . . . |
| she weeps . . . | *flet . . .* |

[61 : 79, 81]

By the bride's side and turned toward her is a second female figure whose head is crowned with a myrtle wreath, from which a robe falls in loose folds, leaving the upper part of her body uncovered. This figure is Venus, and in the picture she represents comfort and encouragement. Her left arm encircles the bride's shoulders; with her right hand she makes an eloquent gesture as if to emphasize the words Catullus has her say:

| | |
|---|---|
| Weep no more! Not to you, | *Flere desine! Non tibi,* |
| Aurunculeia, is there danger | *Aurunculeia, periculum est,* |
| that any fairer woman | *ne qua femina pulcrior* |
| shall see the bright day | *clarum ab Oceano diem* |
| coming from the Ocean. | *viderit venientem.* |

[61 : 86–90]

The timidity and doubt of the one woman are splendidly contrasted with the dignity and assurance of the other.

In front of these seated women and farther to the left stands a third, who obviously belongs to the circle of the goddess of love. Her left arm rests on a small column; her green robe has fallen to her hips, leaving the upper part of her body bare. With her right hand she pours scented oil from a little bottle into a shell in her left hand. Pensively, she gazes at the bride, for whom she symbolizes grace and beauty. Catullus makes this clear in a metaphor in the next lines of his poem:

| | |
|---|---|
| So in the gay garden | *Talis in vario solet* |
| of a rich owner | *divitis domini hortulo* |
| stands a hyacinth flower. | *stare flos hyacinthinus.* |

[61 : 91–93]

Opposite her, at the head of the bed, a deeply tanned youth lolls in a relaxed pose (plates 12, 13). A wreath of ivy leaves dotted with red and yellow flowers adorns his curly hair. He is looking at the two women on the couch as if he expected them to do something. Catullus alludes to him in the passage describing the bride:

| | |
|---|---|
| Noble shame delays: | *Tardat ingenuus pudor:* |
| yet listening rather to this, | *quem tamen magis audiens* |
| she weeps that she must go. | *flet, quod ire necesse est.* |

[61 : 79–81]

This suggests who the youth is meant to be: the bridegroom's attendant or the best man, as he would be called today. In the poem he is called Hymen Hymenaeus, the god of marriage. But the wreath is an attribute of Bacchus, who is sometimes identified as the father of Hymenaeus, sometimes as Hymenaeus himself. Be that as it may, the youth in the painting is the best man, dressed in Dionysian attire, awaiting a signal from the bride to lead her to the bridegroom, as custom demanded.

On the right, outside the house, stand three girls. One is strumming on a lyre while another, whose head is adorned with a tall crown, waits for the note on which to start singing the nuptial chant. The third is busying herself about a large basin in the shape of a *thymiaterion* or incense burner. In fact, the marriage ceremony began in the bride's home with a sacrifice, the dedication of toys, dolls, and locks of hair, and—last but not least—the drawing of the bath water and the ritual ablutions. This part of the ceremony is represented at the other end of the picture, inside the house. Beside a large basin of water set on a circular base stands a majestic female figure, presumably the bride's mother. She is preparing the bridal bath with the assistance of a boy and a girl.

It seems natural to view the *Aldobrandini Wedding* as a picture sequence describing part of the traditional course of the marriage ceremony. Catullus' occasional poem followed a long series of Greek models that culminated in the works of the great lyric poetess Sappho in the sixth century B.C. The figures of the fresco seem also to derive from conventional types known to us from Greek sculptures of the preceding centuries; but here we find them in a different context and imbued with new life. As a result, the homely occasional picture—inspired by the same spirit as Catullus' poem—has reached a pitch of perfection that only in the days of Augustan classicism could have been achieved with such facility. This facility and the light touch with which the skillful artist painted the picture on the wall were noted by Goethe. "To enjoy it and be able to discuss its qualities and defects is a very stimulating and instructive pastime," he wrote to the publisher Johann Friedrich Cotta on October 17, 1797.

*G.D.*

8 Detail from the *Aldobrandini Wedding:* Musicians ▷

9 *The Aldobrandini Wedding;* Roman fresco

10 Detail: Venus and the Bride ▷

12 Detail: Venus and the Bride, with Attendant Groomsman

13 Detail: The Groomsman ▷

14 Detail: A Bridesmaid, or Charis

# 3 Picture Frieze with Scenes from the *Odyssey*

"Ulysses' wanderings from one place to another" *(Ulixis errationes per topia)* is one of the themes for mural decoration mentioned by Vitruvius in his *De Architectura* (book 7, chapter 5: 2). That we can see today what an experiment of this sort looked like at the time is owing to a lucky discovery made on the Esquiline Hill in Rome in the year 1848.

The frieze adorned the upper part of a wall. It is unique, for nothing like it has ever been found before or since. Through the painted architectural frame we look out over a heroic landscape. The *trompe-l'œil* pillars—red with gilded capitals and architrave—divide the frieze into various fields. The pillars are arranged in two rows, one behind the other, as if those of the back row were the shadows of those in front. In the first four pictures (plates 15–18) we see the back pillars to the left of the front ones; in the last two pictures (plates 20, 21), to their right; and in the fifth (plate 19), one to the left and one to the right. Hence this fifth picture occupied the center of the frieze. From the report of the find we know that only one section is missing from the left-hand edge of the frieze; it was destroyed during the digging operations. In all probability the frieze consisted of eleven sections with scenes from the *Odyssey*. Six have come down to us entire, plus a seventh that is only half as wide as the others.

The center section (plate 19) represents the courtyard of Circe's palace. In the left-hand section we see the island of the Laestrygonians, a grandiose landscape with cliffs and the sea. The right-hand section takes us to the shores of the underworld. The adventures of the long-suffering Ulysses in the land of the Laestrygonians, in Circe's palace, and on his way to the underworld are depicted exactly as described by Homer, who is now presumed to have lived in the eighth century B.C., in Books 10 and 11 of the *Odyssey*. To remove any possible doubt as to the identity of the *dramatis personae*, the painter went so far as to write their names in Greek letters alongside most of the figures.

The first picture (plate 15) shows Ulysses and his comrades newly arrived in the land of the Laestrygonians. Several ships are riding at anchor in the bay. This is how Homer describes the scene in Alexander Pope's translation:

> Within a long recess a bay there lies,
> Edged round with cliffs high pointing to the skies.
> [10: 101–102]

Above the ships we see winged creatures flying in the clouds. They are the winds, which drove the ships hither after they had been set free by Ulysses' comrades. The latter out of curiosity opened the pipe their leader had received as a gift from Aeolus. The missing field to the left of the frieze may have represented Ulysses' adventure on the island of Aeolus.

In the center foreground a woman of gigantic stature greets three men Ulysses sent to reconnoiter. The scene is described by Homer in the following lines:

> When lo! they met, beside a crystal spring,
> The daughter of Antiphates the king;
> She to Artacia's silver streams came down.
>
> [10: 119–121]

The nymph is portrayed standing beside a dark grotto-like opening; the painter designated her as "Krene," which means spring. To the right are sheep and cattle, whose herdsmen we can see with other herds in the next picture.

The second scene (plate 16) begins bucolically in the land of the Laestrygonians, "where the shepherd, quitting here at night the plain, / calls, to succeed his cares, the watchful swain" [10: 94–95]. But further on the eager activities of the gigantic, dark-skinned inhabitants become truly hair-raising. One tears down boughs and trees; others lift up heavy rocks. In their midst stands Antiphates, the king, urging them on with eloquent gestures:

> Balk'd of his prey, the yelling monster flies,
> And fills the city with his hideous cries:
> A ghastly band of giants hear the roar,
> And, pouring down the mountains, crowd the shore.
> Fragments they rend from off the craggy brow
> And dash the ruins on the ships below.
>
> [10: 135–140]

A dreadful fate threatens to break over the heads of Ulysses' comrades.

The catastrophe is depicted in all its horror in the third section of the frieze (plate 17):

> The crackling vessels burst; hoarse groans arise,
> And mingled horrors echo to the skies;
> The men like fish, they struck upon the flood,
> And cramm'd their filthy throats with human food.
>
> [10: 121–124]

The scene is set in a broad bay enclosed by steep cliffs, forming a natural harbor.

In the fourth section (plate 18) the island of the Laestrygonians lies at the left. In the foreground a Laestrygonian is massacring a Greek. Ulysses' ship is emerging under full sail from behind a beetling crag: that man of many wiles had left it at anchor in the open sea outside the bay and so it had escaped destruction. Homer says:

> But the sad fate that did our friends destroy,
> Cool'd every breast, and damp'd the rising joy.
>
> [10: 155–156]

It is not until we reach the next section, the fifth (plate 19), that we know with certainty whither the ship was heading. That section shows us the courtyard of Circe's palace. This is how Ulysses himself describes the scene:

> Arrived, before the lofty gates I stay'd;
> The lofty gates the goddess wide display'd:
> She leads before, and to the feast invites;
> I follow sadly to the magic rites.
>
> [10: 341–344]

Ulysses and Circe reappear in the middle of the courtyard, before the pillared porch of the palace. He is seated; she kneels before him. Here too Homer lets Ulysses tell the story in his own words:

> Radiant with starry studs, a silver seat
> Received my limbs; a footstool eased my feet.
>
> [10: 345–346]

Circe's aim is to change the hero into a swine by touching him with her magic wand and then to lock him up in a sty, as she has already done his comrades. But he, made immune to her spells by a herb he had received from Hermes, attacks her with his sword. Whereupon Circe endeavors to win his confidence with words of love, but he insists that his comrades must be released before he yields to her demands.

The sixth section of the fresco is still extant, but the paintwork is so ruined that one can only guess at the end of the encounter with Circe and whither Ulysses' wanderings took him next.

In the seventh section (plate 20) Ulysses' ship has reached the shore of Hades. Ulysses himself has passed through the opening in the cliff and descended into the underworld, to the tranquil waters of the Styx. Wearing his helmet and carrying his drawn sword in his right hand, he advances in the dusky gloom toward the thronging dead who appear on the right:

> When lo! the mighty Theban I behold;
> To guide his steps he bore a staff of gold.
>
> [11: 112–113]

The focal point of the picture is the meeting with Tiresias, because from him Ulysses learned what fate still held in store:

> Why, mortal, wanderest thou from cheerful day,
> To tread the downward, melancholy way?
>
> [11: 116–117]

The last section that has been preserved (plate 21) shows some of the torments of the underworld. It is only half as wide as the others but should be complete because the excavator's report says that it adjoined an opening in the wall. The picture is overshadowed by a huge, menacing crag, atop which Orion pursues his endless hunt armed with mace and sling. On the slope Sisyphus tries in vain to reach the summit with his rock. Beneath the overhang Tityus lies fettered on the ground while ravenous vultures devour his liver for ever. Homer tells us about them all. In the foreground we see the Danaids toiling under their water pitchers, which they empty into a tub that never fills.

The cycle must have been completed with other scenes from Ulysses' wanderings. Not long ago attention was called to a fragment of fresco in the Museo delle Terme, formerly in a private collection, which undoubtedly once formed part of the frieze. It refers to the episode of the sirens.

15 Detail from the Odyssey Frieze: The Arrival of Ulysses in the Land of the Laestrygonians

As far as the course of events is concerned, the painter has kept very close to Homer's narrative, though in some of the scenes the action is rather dramatized. But what really interested him was to render the imaginary landscape with its cliffs, bays, trees, and sea. The mural owes its charm to the combination of this spreading landscape in deep perspective and the nimble little figures engaged in clearly decipherable action. The friezelike painting with its Greek inscriptions is obviously copied from a Hellenistic model. The addition of the pillars divided it more or less arbitrarily into a series of pictures with views that extend to the far distance. In this way Roman spaciousness has given the Greek picture frieze a third dimension. A Roman of the late Republican period about the middle of the first century B.C. may have commissioned it for the monumental decoration of his home. In the passage of his book on architecture quoted at the beginning of this chapter, Vitruvius called his fellow citizens at that period of his country's history *antiqui*, that is, people of olden times.

*G.D.*

16 Detail: The Laestrygonians in Camp

17 Detail: The Laestrygonians Hurling Rocks at the Fleet of Ulysses

18 Detail: Ulysses' Ship Escaping from the Laestrygonians

19 Detail: Ulysses in Circe's Palace ▷

20 Detail: Ulysses in the Underworld ▷

# 4 Glassware and Cut Stones

In ancient times, glass was one of the most precious materials. Symptomatic of its value is an anecdote related by Petronius, the emperor Nero's master of ceremonies, in the fiftieth and following chapters of his *Satyricon*. Trimalchio boasts that he owns some genuine Corinthian bronzes and adds, "But I prefer glass. If it weren't so fragile, I would like glass better than gold." He goes on to tell the following story: A craftsman who had made an unbreakable glass goblet was brought with it into the presence of the emperor. Pretending to hand it to his ruler, the glassmaker let the goblet fall to the floor instead. The emperor was speechless with dismay. But the glass was only slightly dented; the craftsman took a hammer from his pocket and soon set the damage to rights. He felt like a god when the emperor asked him, "Can anyone besides you make glass of this sort?" "No one," he replied. So the emperor had him beheaded for fear that his glassware would become valueless if the secret of the new glass was found out.

The respect in which glassmakers were held in those days is proved by the fact that they signed their works and also by the privileges they enjoyed in the matter of taxation. These craftsmen were freed from all levies so that they might have time to improve their technical skill and to devote themselves to the training of the rising generation.

The discovery of glass dates back to the fourth millennium B.C. According to the Elder Pliny, a scholar who lived during the first century of our era, it was discovered by chance. This is the story he tells in his *Naturalis historia* (book 36: 191). Some Phoenician sailors, preparing their dinner on the seashore where there were no stones, placed their pot on blocks of soda that formed their ship's cargo. The heat of the fire melted the soda, which combined with the sand that lay underneath to produce streams of a new, transparent liquid.

Actually, glass is obtained by the process of fusing silicic acid and alkali. Silicic acid is a component of pure quartz, and alkali is found in the soda produced by marine plants (sodium carbonate) as well as in potash, which is lixiviated wood ash. Glass made in this way is spontaneously colored by the iron contained in the sand. Deep rich tints are obtained by the admixture of coloring agents in the form of metal oxides. Colorless glass is obtained by adding a very little manganese oxide, which clarifies the molten mass and produces a crystal-clear substance. This process was discovered about the beginning of the Christian era.

In the early days glass was cast. Two methods were used. The first consisted in pouring the molten mass into hollow molds, the second in dipping a clay core into the semifluid mass and modeling its surface. When the glass was cold, it could be finished with a grinding wheel. The invention of the blowpipe toward

◁ 21 Detail: Torments of the Underworld

the end of the first century B.C. brought with it a fundamental change in glassmaking. The new implement offered the possibility of blowing a lump of molten glass into a hollow mold. But it could also be used to form a vessel without a mold; it was on this method that the first experiments in mass production were subsequently based.

From the outset glass was valued as a material for decoration in Mesopotamia and Egypt as well as on Crete and in Mycenae. During the classical age of Greece it seems to have been rather rare. It was employed, however, to adorn Phidias' statue of Zeus, one of the most famous sculptures of antiquity. In the reign of Augustus, Italy became the center of glass manufacture. From there it spread throughout the entire Roman empire. During that period a glass industry developed in the Rhineland, which exported its products even to Rome. A quantity of the glassware produced there, from the simplest to the most elaborate, has come down tu us.

Only a few specimens from the rich collection of antique glass in the Vatican Library can be reproduced here; they date from the late years of the Roman empire. Plate 23 shows fourteen blown-glass vessels of various shapes and sizes that were very common from the first to the fourth century of our era. Most of them are *balsamaria*, small containers for unguents or perfumes. The beautiful iridescent sheen is the result of a superficial patina produced by weathering in the course of time; it is not due to the makers' intention.

The bell-shaped goblet in plate 22 was also blown into a mold. The marine animals were modeled separately and stuck on the outside of the vessel before the glass was cold. The colored composition of shells and fish gives this work a peculiar charm.

Plates 24 and 25 reproduce two specimens of glasses blown into molds with incised figural decoration. A small grinding wheel was employed with sand and water to cut the cold glass. On one (plate 24), the emphasis is on the delicate plastic modeling of the figures. On the other (plate 25), the designs are defined by contour lines and a few details of the inner drawing. The first is decorated with a religious theme—the Glorification of Christ; the second with a secular motif—fishermen with their boats and nets.

Virtually all precious and semiprecious stones were known and worked in the earliest times. The most common were chalcedony and agate; the rarer rock crystal was used less frequently. On gems the figural representation was first drawn, then cut, bored, and polished; the process, forming a kind of relief in reverse, is called intaglio. In cameos, instead, the relief is raised; the artist carves his design in a hard, multicolored stone, taking clever advantage of the layers and veins of different colors.

The two rectangular plaques of rock crystal reproduced in plates 27 and 28 were worked after the manner of gems. The designs have a still-life quality. It is not known what these plaques were used for; they may have served as distinguishing marks on graves. The fish was a favorite symbol in early Christian times and is frequently met with in the catacombs. The letters of the Greek word for fish *(ICHTHYS)* are at the same time the initials of the words *Iēsous CHristos THeou HYios Sōtēr* (Jesus Christ Son of God Saviour). So it is natural to find the fish as a recurring motif in early Christian art. Clement of Alexandria, the great teacher and humanist of the early third century, said that things which called to mind wealth and luxury were not suitable for Christians: "Our emblems should rather represent a dove or a fish."

Plates 26 and 29 give a good idea of cameo work. The latter shows a piece of light-brown agate. Although only a small fragment has been preserved, the head can be identified beyond question as that of Augustus, of whom a bronze portrait head is reproduced in plate 3. This cameo is an example of the high level attained in this art form. By way of contrast, the chalcedony masks termed *phalerae* reproduced in plate 28 were occasional works of little artistic value—badges or amulets meant to be worn on a string.

*G.D.*

22 Glass goblet with applied fish and shells ▷

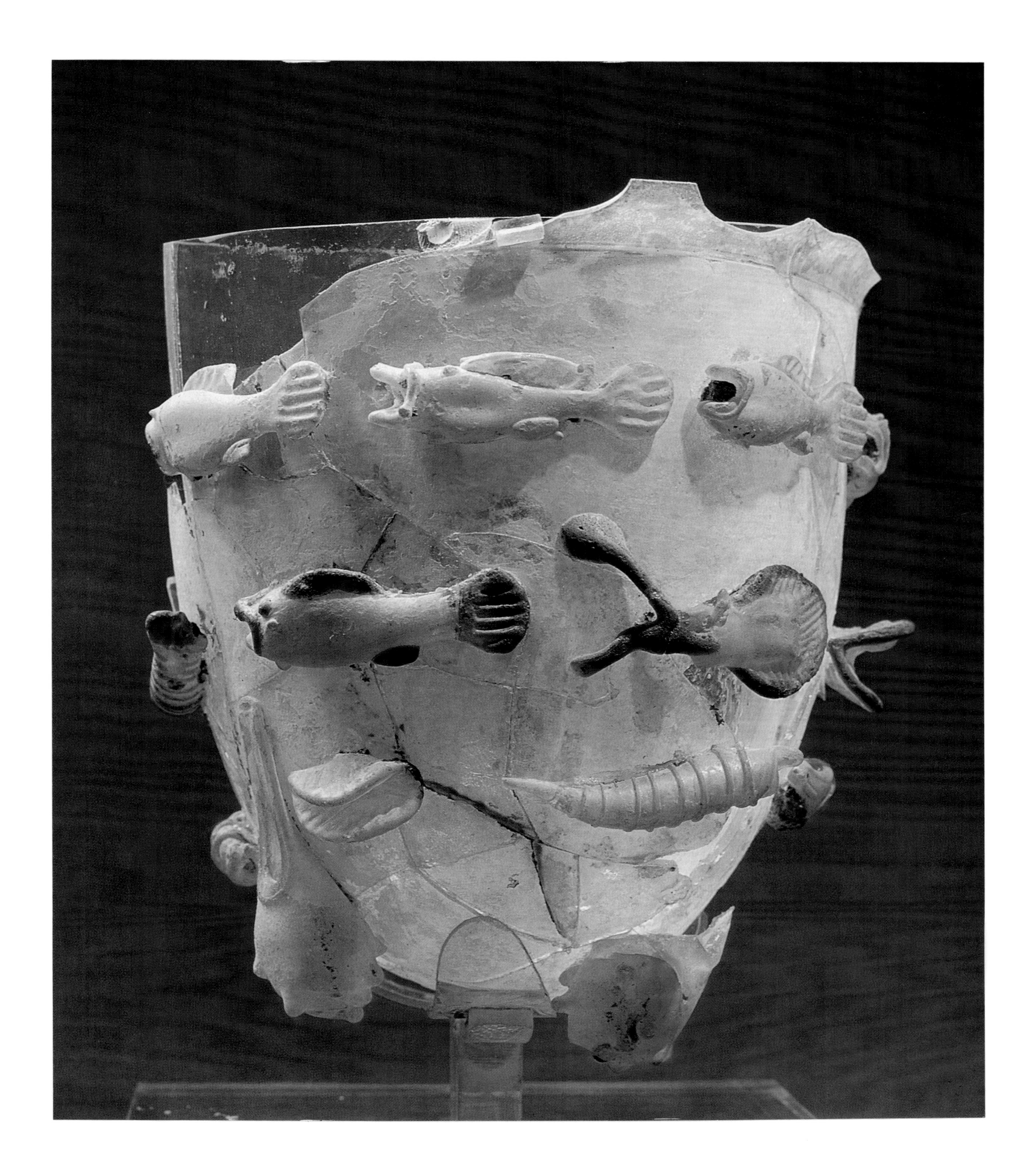

23 Fourteen small glass bottles: balsamaria, ampullae, bowls, and pitchers ▷

24 Fragment of a shallow cut-glass bowl with a scene of the Glorification of Christ

25 Small semi-spherical cut glass with fishing scenes ▷

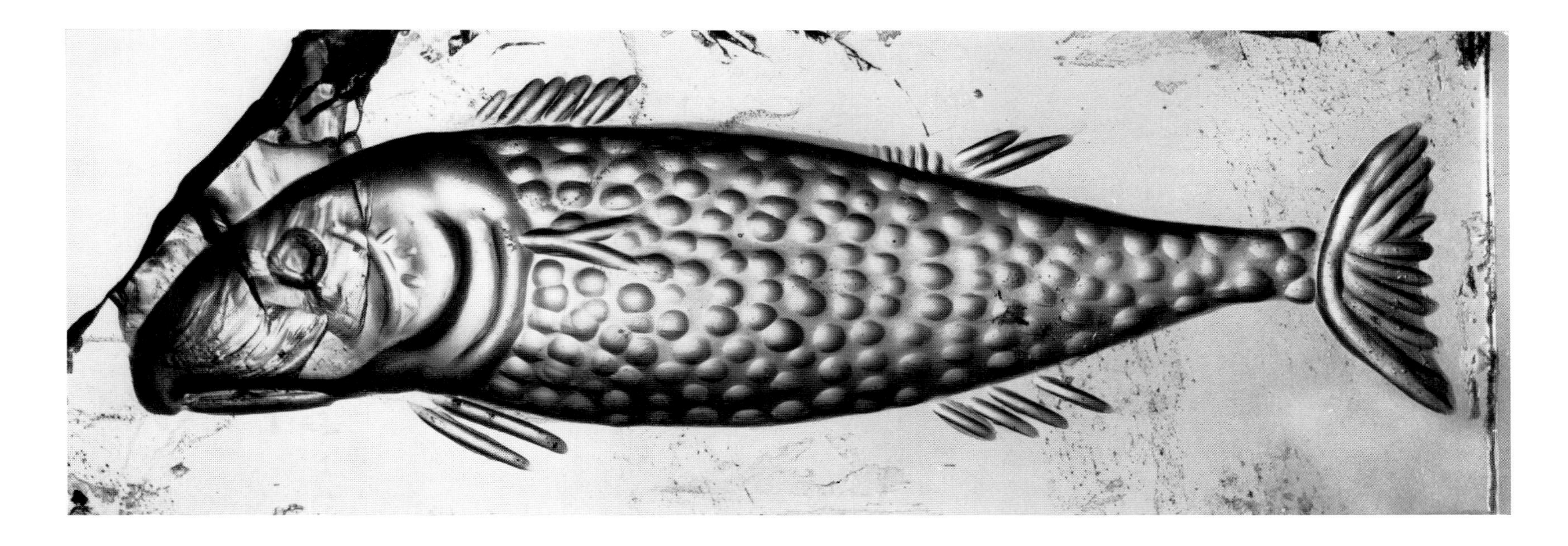

◁ 26 Seven chalcedony *phalerae* or mask-shaped badges

27 Cut rock-crystal plate with fish

28 Cut rock-crystal plate with goat under a tree

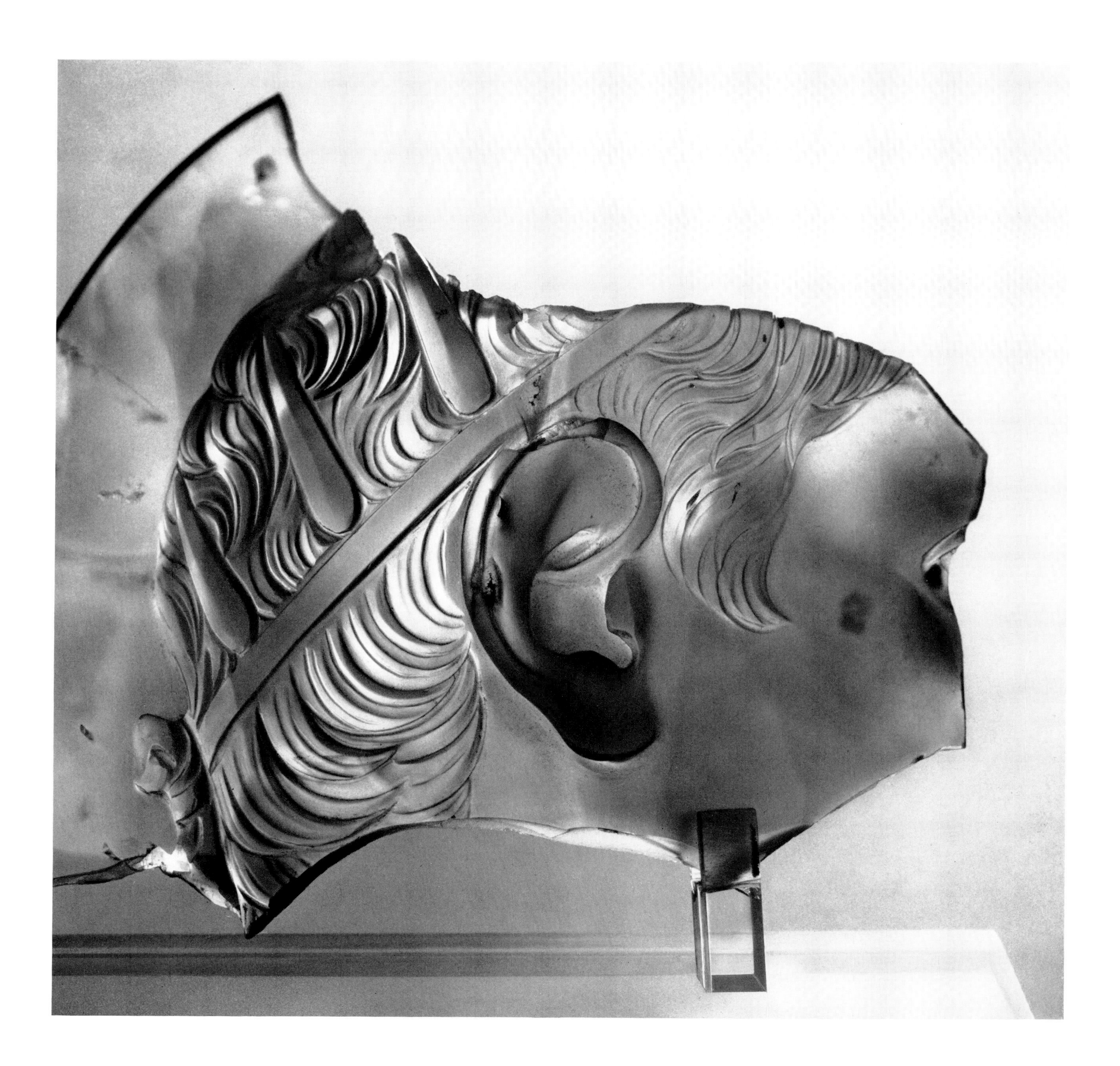

29 Fragment of cameo with head of the emperor Augustus

# 5 Gold Glass

The Museo Sacro of the Vatican Library contains the world's largest collection of antique gold glasses, which are also called *fondi d'oro* (gold bottoms) since entire vessels in this medium have, in fact, never yet been discovered. Gold glasses are pictures in the shape of circular plates that usually show signs of breakage around the rim, indicating that at one time they were the bases of drinking vessels or bowls; some, however, are medallions with smooth rim. They are made of two flat or slightly concave layers of glass separated by a filmy piece of gold leaf. Decorative motifs, inscriptions, or human or animal figures were engraved in the foil with a burin; the superfluous metal was then removed so that the bottom glass appeared as a background. This glass is always colored—either blue, green, or brown—whereas the top glass is usually colorless.

We can visualize the method by which these gold glasses were produced. The gold-leaf picture was placed on a circle of glass blown with a pipe. To prevent damage it was covered with a film of molten glass. Then the top glass, which was also blown, was applied, forming a thin, transparent skin. Thus the gold was completely sealed in glass. The top glass had a slightly upturned rim, which was broken off when the glass was cold. When reheated, the rough edge formed a ring, which is often taken for the base ring on which the glass rested. The bottom glass was also broken off around the rim more or less skillfully. For small medallions a drop of molten glass was poured onto the gold leaf, thus sealing the picture.

Heraclius, a tenth-century writer who admired ancient Rome to the point of viewing it as a lost paradise, relates in his treatise *De coloribus et artibus Romanorum* (On the Colors and Arts of the Romans) his attempts to copy gold glasses *(de fialis auro decoratis)*.

> Wonderful dishes of glass, to be praised as precious above all else, were ingeniously prepared by the Romans and adorned with gold. . . . There I found leaves of beaten gold carefully enclosed between double glass, and the more I contemplated this with an inventive spirit, the more stimulated I felt. I procured several dishes of bright sparkling glass and spread them with a brush dipped in resin. When I had done this I began to put the gold leaves on the golden dishes, and when I saw they were dry I scratched little birds thereon and shells, little flowers and lions, just as struck my fancy. Then to protect the dishes I covered them with thin layers of glass blown in the fire. And as soon as this glass had felt the heat uniformly I sealed it thinly around the dishes in first-rate fashion.

Heraclius was unacquainted with the workshop tradition of the ancient glassmakers. This makes his report, couched in hexameters,

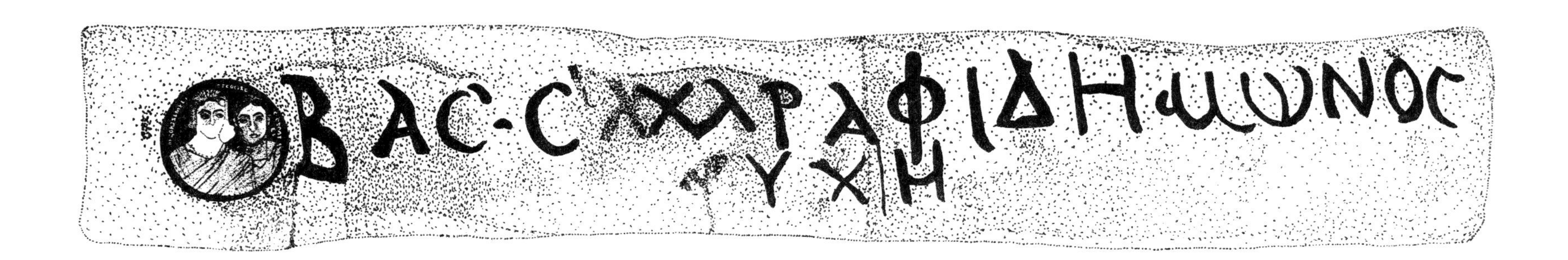

all the more worthy of admiration, for it shows great understanding and gives a vivid idea of the manufacturing process.

All the Roman gold glasses were found in the catacombs, the majority by antiquaries between the sixteenth and eighteenth centuries. Unfortunately, exact details of most of the finds are not known, although it is assumed that the glasses were used primarily if not exclusively as grave markers. Such indeed was the case with one of the few glasses found and recorded *in situ:* the portrait medallion of a man and his wife reproduced in plate 34. This plaque was pressed into the roughcast that sealed a wall grave *(loculus)* in the catacomb of Pamphilus. Alongside it was the inscription in Greek characters, painted in red, shown in the linecut at the top of this page. The inscription reads: "Bassa, beloved, Philemon's soul." There seems to be no connection between this epitaph and the words, as yet uninterpreted, in Latin letters on the glass.

Plate 38 provides a good example of a gold glass still embedded in the original roughcast. The slightly protuberant circular rim of the upper layer, presumably the base of the entire glass when intact, here served a further useful purpose: it marked the limit to which the plaster was to be laid on, covering the jagged edges of the glass and framing the roundel.

The pictures on gold glasses differ widely. Most of them bear no reference to religion although they were found in Christian catacombs. Portraits were a favorite theme. Gold glasses with portraits are not only the oldest but also the finest examples of this art form. Some of the portraits are full length, for instance that of Dedalius (plate 30). Others are busts, like that of Eusebius (plate 33). Some represent married couples or entire families (plates 34, 35, 37). Secular themes include animals and hunting scenes (plates 31, 39). The depiction of a Nereid seated on a fabulous beast with the front part of a stag and the tail of a fish (plate 38) was probably derived from ancient imagery. Gold glasses with Christian representations show a quantity of scenes from the Old and New Testaments and portraits of saints (plates 40, 42–44, 49, 50); among the latter, the Apostles Peter and Paul are particularly frequent (plates 45–48). The medallion reproduced in plate 32 is linked with the Jewish faith. In the upper half two lions guard the Torah shrine (in which the scrolls are kept); in the lower section are two seven-branched candelabra and other ritual objects.

The inscriptions on the gold glasses, besides invoking people's names, are mostly toasts. The mixture of Latin and Greek gives rise to odd forms, such as the *pie, zeses* (drink, mayst thou live) on the Dedalius portrait glass. The inscription *Hilaris vivas cum tuis feliciter semper refrigeris in pace dei* (Hilarius, live happily with yours, find comfort for ever in the peace of God) on plate 42 is the only one unequivocally Christian in character; this is confirmed by the addition of the monogram of Christ. The discovery of this glass in the Roman catacombs links it with the cult of the departed.

The gold glasses reproduced in this book date from the late period of the Roman empire, from the third to the fifth century. They reflect very clearly the difference in mentality and attitude between paganism and Christianity. They also show that both could live side by side and that ancient images could be given a Christian interpretation. Insofar as the Christian images are concerned, the stereotyped forms soon adopted for certain conceptions were frequently borrowed from the ancient tradition. The figure of the Praying woman (plate 51, top) is identified by the inscription AGNES; hence it expresses the Christian trust in Salvation. In the pagan context the same figure symbolizes *pietas* in the religio-cultic sense. This shows how the subject of a picture may be given a new meaning—in a word, Christianized. The same applies to the picture of Moses striking water from the rock (plate 51, bottom). Its meaning is changed by the inscription PETRUS: Moses' function in the Old Testament is assumed by Peter in the New Testament.

*G.D.*

30 Gold glass with portrait of the shipbuilder Dedalius and carpenters at work in a shipyard ▷

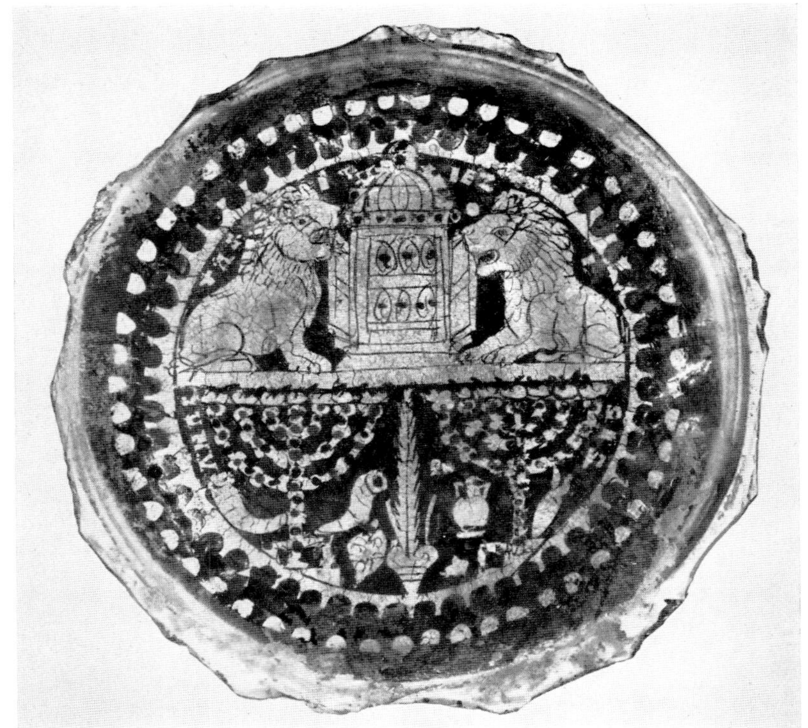

31 Gold glass with galloping ass

32 Gold glass with Jewish religious objects and two lions

33 Gold-glass medallion with portrait of Eusebius

34 Gold-glass medallion with portraits of a man and a woman

35 Gold-glass medallion with family portrait

36 Gold-glass medallion with portrait of a boy

37 Gold glass with portraits of a man and a woman

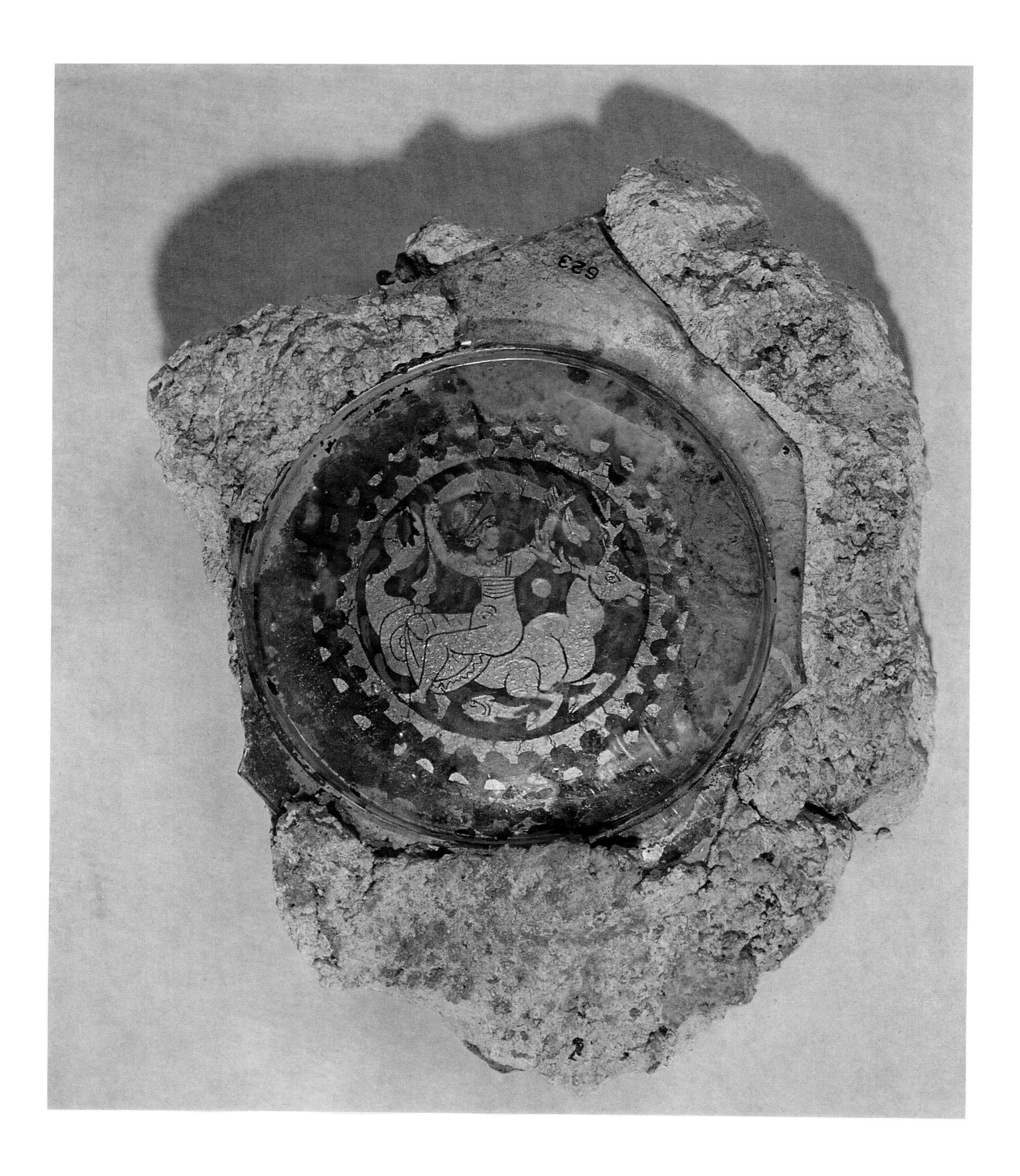

◁ 38 Gold glass in wall plaster, with Nereid on a fabulous beast

39 Gold glass with hunting scene

40 Gold glass with the Raising of Lazarus and the Miracle at Cana

41 Gold glass with seven busts and one full-length figure

42 Gold glass with Saints Lawrence and Cyprian

43 Gold glass with the Raising of Lazarus

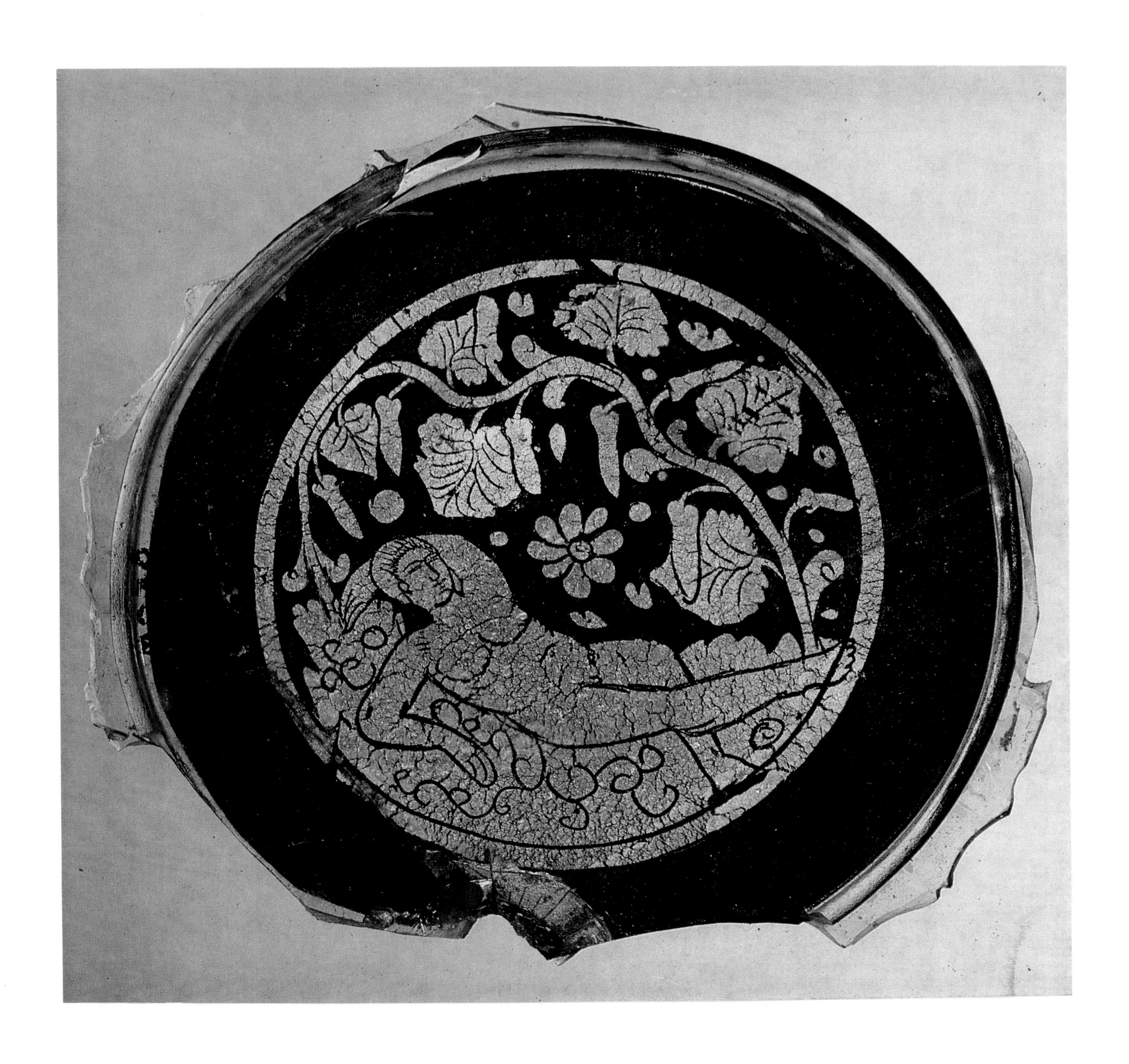

44 Gold glass with Jonah Resting Under the Gourd

45 Gold glass with Saints Peter and Paul

46 Gold glass with Saint Paul

47 Gold glass with Saints Peter and Paul and a crown of oak leaves

48 Gold glass with Saints Peter and Paul and garlands

◁ 49 Seventeen small gold glasses with scenes from the Old and New Testaments

50 Eight gold glasses with figurative motifs

751

# 6 Lamps and Silver Vessels

Lamps were the commonest lighting devices in ancient times, and innumerable specimens have been preserved. Their design was simple in the extreme and varied but slightly until the late antique period. Lamps were employed not only in the home but also for devotional use. The early Christians adopted the traditional shape, and their lamps can be distinguished from pagan ones only when specifically Christian symbols were used for adornment (plate 52). The miles of catacombs required an immense number of lamps for the use of visitors and for graveside ceremonies.

The light was produced by a burning wick. The fuel was either oil or tallow. For that reason an antique lamp, in its basic form, comprises a fuel container, usually in the shape of a small round or oval bowl, on which are fitted one or more spouts or nozzles for the wick. Handles, stands, or suspension devices are added and may be embellished with ornaments (plates 52 and 57).

Clay was the material most commonly used for making lamps, but metal, usually bronze, was also employed. Bronze lamps were cast and the decorative plates on the handle soldered on later. In the case of clay lamps, the upper and lower parts were fashioned separately in suitable molds and put together afterwards, the seam being smoothed out with a modeling tool. In this way clay lamps could be mass-produced; the maker's name was stamped on the bottom.

The distinguishing mark of a lamp is the ornamentation. Space for this was provided by the circular upper face of the fuel container, in which holes were bored for pouring in the oil and allowing the air to escape. In bronze lamps the filling hole is usually closed with a hinged lid; the major decorative element is the plate soldered onto the handle.

Many of the ornamental motifs are based on a long tradition. The theme of the sheep or ram carrier (plate 53) occurs in votive statuettes during the archaic period as early as the seventh century B.C. In the pagan world of the Roman empire it was the symbol of *philanthropia;* for the Christians it became the Good Shepherd, which is found in the New Testament as an allegory of Christ. The peacock (plate 56) was one of the animals sacred to Dionysus in ancient times. In the Roman empire the bird became the symbol of astral immobility because of the starlike designs on its tail; its function was to carry the female members of the imperial family into the other world. The Christians viewed the peacock as the bird of paradise—the symbol of resurrection and eternal life. The significance of the theme of the watcher's hut in the vineyard (plate 55) is explained in literary terms in *De montibus Sina et Sidon*, a pseudo-Cyprianic treatise dating from the first half of the third century of our era: When the grapes are ripe and the harvest approaches, a boy is placed as a watcher in a tall tree in

◁ 51 Two gold glasses: Saint Agnes as Orant, and Saint Peter Striking Water from a Rock

the midst of the vineyard. Thus Christ watches over His people from the vantage point of the Cross to see that the devil does not injure anyone or lure him from the Lord's vineyard. The figure of Jonah (plates 44 and 54) is also an allusion to the themes of Redemption and Salvation: after being swallowed up by a great fish and vomited out on the dry land three days later, he rests on a couch under a gourd.

The decorative plates on bronze lamps are adorned with Christian emblems—for example, Christ's monogram (plate 52), which recalls Constantine's banner, the *labarum*, or the Latin cross (plate 57).

In antiquity silver was highly prized, not only because it was particularly well suited for minting coins. More important were the utensils and tableware made by silversmiths, references to which in literary sources have been amply confirmed by archaeological discoveries. The finds at Boscoreale and in the House of Menander at Pompeii, which was covered by volcanic débris when Vesuvius erupted in A.D. 79, have become famous. But other buried treasures comprising valuable Roman silverware have also come to light not only in Rome itself but also at Hildesheim (Germany), Hoby (Denmark), Mildenhall (England), Berthouville (France), Augst (Switzerland), and Concesti (Rumania), to mention but a few of the most important.

To get an idea of the wealth of the late antique and early Christian periods, one has merely to glance through the *Liber Pontificalis*. That work is a history of the popes in the form of a succession of biographies in chronological order from the first century to the sixth, with later supplements. It mentions a very large number of artistic objects in metal that were either donated to various churches by the popes or received by them as gifts from other sovereigns; for instance, those which Pope Hormisdas (514–23) received from the Byzantine emperor Justinus. Few of these objects have been preserved; of those still extant, some are kept in the Museo Sacro.

Most of the silverware consists of reliquaries and other objects for ritual use, but secular articles have also found their way into the museum. One is a large silver dish which measures almost sixteen inches in diameter (plate 58). The motif embossed in the center after the manner of a medallion represents a boar hunt. The hunter mounted on a galloping horse aims his spear at a large wild boar that is charging him from the undergrowth. Lower down is a hound running by his master's side. There are many references in the literature and art of antiquity to hunting the wild boar of Calydonia, which cost Meleager his life. Obviously this silver dish has no connection with that myth. In fact, it was very likely executed in honor of a nobleman who lived during the fifth or sixth century of our era.

The ornamentation of the two silver vessels reproduced in plate 59 is proof of their Christian origin: in the roundels are portraits of Christ and the Apostles. On the pitcher the theme is repeated in allegorical form: above the row of roundels, the Cross flanked by doves; beneath it, a lamb among sheep.

The small oval silver box reproduced in plates 60 and 61 was found in the altar of the basilica of Henchir Zirara, Algeria; this proves that it was a receptacle for the relics of saints. Saint Polycarp was the first martyr whose bones are known to have been collected by the community and considered "more valuable than precious stones." On the lid of the little box the saint of Henchir Zirara is portrayed flanked by two lighted tapers in candlesticks and holding a martyr's crown in his hands; at his feet flow the four rivers of paradise; above his head God's hand appears from amid the clouds conferring on him the crown of eternal life (plate 61). On the side of the box (plate 60) a stag and hind symbolize yearning for the Lord, an allusion to Psalm 41:1–2: "As the hart panteth after the fountains of water, so my soul panteth after Thee, O God." Kneeling down, the animals drink the water of the four rivers, above which appears the emblem of Christ. The palms at either side symbolize the promised land.

Purely ornamental, instead, is the efect given by the pattern on the pyxlike vessel (plate 62) in which the church of the Santi Quattro Coronati formerly preserved the head of Saint Sebastian. The inscription tells us that the reliquary was donated by Pope Gregory IV (827–44). Here on the threshold of the Middle Ages, after an unbroken tradition of over a thousand years, the palmette and acanthus leaf motif, which was first used as ornamentation in classical Greek art, achieves a new urgency.

*G.D.*

52 Bronze oil lamp with two spouts and suspension device; ornamented with Christ's monogram ▷

53
Terracotta oil lamp with the Good Shepherd

54
Terracotta oil lamp with Jonah Under the Gourd

55
Terracotta oil lamp with watcher's hut in vineyard

56
Terracotta oil lamp with peacock

57
Bronze oil lamp with suspension device ▷

58 Silver dish with wild boar hunt

59 Two silver vessels with Apostle medallions

60 Oval silver reliquary; side view showing figurative reliefs

61 Lid of silver reliquary (plate 60), with figure of Saint Polycarp ▷

62 Silver and niello reliquary decorated with stylized palmettes and acanthus leaves

# 7 The Treasure of the Sancta Sanctorum Chapel

The Papal Palace of the Lateran was the residence of the bishops of Rome until the popes returned from Avignon in 1377. Today it has disappeared. The present Lateran Palace, a Renaissance building erected by Domenico Fontana alongside the Basilica of Saint John, covers a far smaller area. The original papal residence even encompassed the Scala Santa or sacred stairway, where its traces can still be recognized in spite of the alterations made under Sixtus V (1585–90). Famous above all is an almost square chamber at the top of the stairway where precious relics were kept (plate 63); for centuries this chapel has been known as the Sancta Sanctorum (Holy of Holies). First mentioned in the eighth or ninth, it served originally as the pope's private oratory, a function the Sistine Chapel in the Vatican performs today. It was dedicated to Saint Lawrence, the first treasurer and archivist of the Roman Church.

The name of the founder is not known; Pope Silvester (314–35) is to be excluded for historical reasons. All we know for certain is that the chapel is mentioned in the *Liber Pontificalis* in the life of Stephen III (768–72) and perhaps also in those of Sergius I (687–701) and Stephen II (752–57). It long served, after the election of a new pope, as the stopping place of the triumphal procession that led from the chapel of Saint Silvester, located between the Battistero and the Basilica, to the Lateran Palace.

From the very outset the Chapel of Saint Lawrence was employed for religious worship on special occasions and holy days. For on the altar stood, and still stands (plate 63), the image of the Redeemer which was held to be the genuine portrait (in Greek, *acheiropoietos* = not done by human hand) of Christ and is first mentioned in the reign of Stephen II. Some scholars believe that it was brought to Rome from the Byzantine East at the time of the iconoclastic controversy (726–843), as was the portrait of the Virgin in Santa Maria in Trastevere, which documentary evidence proves to have been revered as early as the seventh century.

The picture has been restored several times. Important alterations were made when the face was surrounded by a metal halo under John X (915–28). Under Alexander III (1159–81) the picture was covered with painted silk fabric on which the original image was reproduced. That is how we see it today. Innocent III (1190–1216) had it covered with a thin plate of silver richly decorated with ornamental and figural motifs in relief and set with gems. The face alone was left bare. On Christ's feet two flaps are arranged. They are divided into four compartments, each of which shows the head of Jesus: (1) as High Priest before an altar in an adoration scene (a favorite motif with the Byzantines); (2) in the Whitsun miracle; (3) during a mass celebrated by Saint Peter; (4) at the adoration of the Agnus Dei. By raising the flaps, one could anoint Christ's feet. Small medallion-like gold plates that could be opened were also fitted over the nail wounds in His hands and side.

In the fifteenth century the two lateral wings were added so that the picture could be closed. They were commissioned by Giacomo (or Nicola) Teoli. The inner face of each wing is adorned with pictures in embossed silver. One shows the donor at the feet of the risen Christ with an inscription explaining the donation. The other seven compartments are decorated with the Annunciation and five saints.

The portrait "not done by human hand" was held in great honor from earliest times and was even credited with miraculous powers. When it was imperative to check the destructive fury of Aistulf, king of the Lombards from 749 to 756, who "like a roaring lion" *(fremens ut leo)* threatened to exterminate the Romans, Pope Stephen II carried the picture on his back in a supplicatory procession.

Among the most revered relics of the Sancta Sanctorum were the heads of Saint Peter and Saint Paul. Urban V (1362–70) removed them and placed them high up in the ciborium of the Lateran Basilica, where they are still kept today. As a result of his initiative, Pope Urban is often portrayed holding the two heads of the saints in his hands.

Since the pontificate of Leo III (795–816), the Chapel of Saint Lawrence has been called the Sancta Sanctorum. This is because Leo is believed to have commissioned the cypress-wood shrine that serves as the base of the altar and bears an inscription with his name and the designation Sancta Sanctorum. It is not certain, however, that the designation really dates from the reign of this pope, for it is inscribed on a separate tablet. The carefully made shrine, which still supports the altar, is enclosed by a massive wrought-iron railing fitted with a double gate on the front.

John the Deacon compiled an inventory of the relics preserved in Pope Leo's shrine. From his account it is apparent that no structural alterations had been made in the Sancta Sanctorum from the time the chapel was instituted to the reign of Alexander III (1159–81). A century later Nicholas III (1277–80) found it in a ruinous condition and had it restored. But he did not touch the portrait of Christ in its silver frame or Leo III's precious shrine. He left the chapel as we see it today. Two porphyry columns with entablature divide it into two unequal parts, the smaller of which forms the Holy of Holies proper with the altar shrine. The restoration was entrusted to an architect who called himself "Magister Cosmatus"; his signature can be seen in the entrance. The rich marble and mosaic decoration of floor and walls—the latter are now concealed by red silk hangings—is rated among the finest examples of what is known as "Cosmati work."

The larger section is covered by a cross-rib vault whose soffits are adorned with the emblems of the four Evangelists, probably executed by an artist belonging to the circle of Filippo Rusuti. Unfortunately, they were painted over tastelessly in the eighteenth century. Rusuti himself was the artist who painted the *Pantokrator*, in a style reminiscent of Cavallini, on the ceiling of the smaller section. It shows Christ in a *nimbus* borne by angels. The image of the Pantokrator or All-Ruler recalls Byzantine art, which originated this inconographic type. Famous examples are Hosios Lukas and Daphni in Greece.

On the rear wall of the Sancta Sanctorum are three lunettes in mosaic. In the middle one, the portraits of Saint Peter and Saint Paul; in the two lateral ones, Saint Agnes and Saint Lawrence. Saint Nicholas and Saint Stephen are portrayed in the lunettes on the side walls.

The upper part of the wall in the larger section is embellished with blind arcades of triple Gothic arches. A base of *pavonazzetto* (a bluish purple marble) supports slender spiral columns that recall the cloisters of San Giovanni in Laterano and other famous Roman cloisters. The arches frame pictures of saints, probably painted over older ones, by Giovanni da Perugia (1478–1544). The lunettes, which are separated by tall windows, have older paintings that refer to the chapel itself or the relics it contains. One, for instance, shows Nicholas III flanked by Saints Peter and Paul presenting a model of the chapel to the "Rex Gloriae," the risen Christ.

Extensive restoration was necessary after the catastrophic devastation perpetrated by the emperor Charles V's mercenaries when they sacked Rome in 1527. There was no possibility, of course, of replacing the reliquaries they plundered or the ornaments they destroyed. Only Leo III's shrine under the altar was spared thanks to its massive wrought-iron railing. A description of the original state of the sacred treasure had been written during the reign of Leo X (1513–21), just a few years before the sack of Rome. It was the last.

Sixtus V (1585–90) emphasized the division of the restored chapel into two parts by having the floor of the smaller section—the actual Holy of Holies, with the portrait of Christ on the reliquary shrine—raised slightly. The inscription in gold letters on the crossbeam atop the porphyry columns that frame the altar runs: NON EST IN TOTO SANCTIOR ORBE LOCUS (There is in all the world no holier place). This pentameter, taken perhaps from an ancient hymn, accords with the solemn dignity of the surroundings.

In 1903 Pope Leo XIII gave special permission to open the shrine. His successor, Pius X, had the ancient reliquaries brought to the Vatican Palace and placed in the care of the Library. New receptacles were made for the relics, which were replaced in the shrine under the altar of the Holy of Holies. In 1934, under Pius XI, the Treasure of the Sancta Sanctorum was exhibited publicly in the newly arranged Museo Sacro. However precious the reliquaries so long preserved in the chapel may be for believers, their artistic value is no less great. The incomparable objects are part of the universal heritage of history and art, revealing the culture and customs of ages past.

Particularly awe-inspiring are the fabrics, garments, and cloths *(brandea)* that once touched the bodies of the saints and were soaked with their blood, thus bearing vivid and poignant testimony to their martyrdom.

The ornaments in gold, ivory, and enamelwork, the gems on the reliquaries, and the fabrics these caskets contained give a unique idea of the skill of the craftsmen who made these objects. They also help to shed light on the activities of the various workshops established in Rome and, to an even greater extent perhaps, in the Byzantine East.

The historical importance of this treasure is still further increased by its mention in the *Liber Pontificalis*. For instance, from the description of the precious objects that belonged to Paschal I (817–24), we learn about the *renovatio* that took place in the seventh and eighth centuries—before the "Carolingian Renaissance"—and the aims which motivated Christianity in the West and left their mark upon its forms.

*A.P.*

63 The Sancta Sanctorum, the papal chapel in the old Lateran Palace, now part of the building housing the Scala Santa ▷

NON·EST·IN·TOTO·SANCTIOR·ORBE·LOCVS
S LAV RENTIVS

64 Lid of an ivory box with Christ Healing the Blind Boy

65 Leaves of a wooden diptych with portraits of Saints Peter and Paul painted in wax

66
Small wooden box with mementos from the Holy Land

67 ▷
Tempera paintings inside the lid of memento box (plate 66)

68 Small oval silver box with embossed reliefs

69 Detail from side of silver box (plate 68): The Head of Christ ▷

70 *Left,* cushion for a now lost reliquary cross; *right,* silver box for cross and cushion

71 The silver box of plate 70, embossed, chased, and gilded

72 Detail of silver box (plate 71): Christ Appears to the Disciples Behind Closed Doors ▷

73 Detail of silver box (plate 71): Noli me tangere

74 Detail of silver box (plate 71): The Supper at Emmaus

◁ 75 Gold and enamel reliquary cross with scenes from the childhood of Christ

76 Detail of gold and enamel cross (plate 75): The Presentation in the Temple, and the Baptism

77 Side view of gold and enamel cross (plate 75), showing the inscription of Pope Paschal I ▷

78 The gold and enamel cross (plate 75) in its silver box

79–81 Three sides of the silver box (plate 78):

79 The Annunciation, the Visitation, the Nativity ▷

80 The Annunciation to the Shepherds, and the Three Magi Following the Star ▷

81 The Adoration of the Magi, and the Presentation in the Temple ▷

◁ 82 Silver reliquary for the head of Saint Praxedes

83 Enamel on gold panel, showing Christ Enthroned Between the Virgin and John the Baptist, on the lid of the silver reliquary (plate 82)

O
MON

◁ 84 Enamel on gold medallion of Saint Simon, on the lid of the silver reliquary (plate 82)

85 Enamel on gold medallion of Saint Thomas, on the lid of the silver reliquary (plate 82)

86 Side view of the silver reliquary (plate 82), with embossed figures of two saints

87 The seal of Pope Nicholas III on the silver reliquary (plate 82)

88 Detail of the silver reliquary (plate 82), with embossed figure of Saint Gregory ▷

89 Painted wood reliquary; *left,* the sliding lid with the figure of Saint John Crysostomus; *right,* the inside of the box, with a recess for a double cross and pictures of Christ, the Virgin, two Archangels, Saint Peter, and Saint Paul

# 8 Antique Woven Fabrics

The production and use of textiles made of wool and flax is of extremely ancient origin. Later people made fabrics of mixed fibers and discovered dyeing. As a result, many-hued stuffs found a place alongside the former monochrome ones.

Pliny relates that the Romans were the first to make clothed statues, differing in this from the Greeks, who preferred nude figures. At this point in Western history cloth ceased to be exclusively a commodity and acquired an aesthetic value. It was connected with the idea of beauty and became an element of the artistic statement. From now on we find fabrics with ornamental patterns.

Ornamentation was the criterion for judging the value of a man's clothes and at the same time the dignity of the wearer. This gave fabrics a certain "ethical" value and made them more highly prized, quite apart from their practical value.

Subsequently, the weaving and dyeing processes were constantly improved. The ornamentation was not merely woven into the fabric, as is the usual method with Gobelin tapestry, but was also applied on it. This method must not, however, be confused with embroidery; it was a branch of the weaver's craft.

Silk was considered the most precious material, for which reason it was imported from China to the Mediterranean regions in ever larger quantities at a very early date. But we know from Vergil and Pliny that the Romans had no clear idea of how silk was made. They thought it was obtained by spinning the leaves in which the silkworms turn into chrysalids. Lack of knowledge did not dampen their enthusiasm for the new fiber, however. Silk garments became increasingly fashionable. Veritable silk routes developed with chains of trading centers in Persia and Syria and in Arabia and Egypt. Tyre, Sidon, Beirut, and Alexandria became important markets for colored stuffs, especially those dyed purple.

This makes it easy to understand that as a rule the ornamentation of fabrics made of pure silk, as well as those of silk mixed with wool and flax, was linked with the places where they were processed. By the sixth century of our era, weaving mills in the narrow sense of the term were flourishing in those marketing centers.

The interest taken in silk in those days is demonstrated by the stories that developed around the material, though some of the tales seem closer to fiction than to fact. Procopius relates that the emperor Justinian sent monks to China with orders to discover the secret of making silk. Bishop Asterius of Amasia in Pontus (d. 410) reproved the vogue for very ornate clothes, condemning all garments that made people look like "painted walls."

Our knowledge of woven fabrics and their use derives not only from a quantity of literary documentation but also from mosaics and miniatures. It is true to say that there was a constant improvement in quality, processing, and ornamentation. Fabrics were employed for ever finer and nobler uses until at last they attained an almost spiritual dignity because they were utilized in the religious domain and for religious purposes.

This development reached its culminating point in the Middle Ages. As the world grew gradually poorer, suffered from the disintegration of the Roman empire, and was ravaged by the barbarian invasions, regard for woven fabrics increased. In Western Europe at least such products testified, even more cogently than other works of art, to man's spiritual essence and the artistic heritage of the past.

That famous collection of papal biographies, the *Liber Pontificalis*, appeared in the sixth century. It was based on older documents which were then arranged organically for the first time and were added to regularly during the ensuing centuries. We are indebted to this work for invaluable information on the importance of textiles. The *Liber Pontificalis* records with almost pedantic precision a sort of inventory of each pope's famous acts. It lauds above all a pope's merits in the matter of adding to the Church's treasures and the ceremonies in Rome's great sanctuaries. Chief among those places of worship were the patriarchal basilicas and the tomb of Saint Peter.

Woven fabrics are given special mention among votive offerings. Their value and quality were judged from their origin: they were explicitly designated as "stuffs from Tyre," "Byzantine purple," "Alexandrian cloth," "fabrics from Cyprus," and "Tartar cloth." So we know that the most renowned cloth manufactures were located in Syria, Byzantium, Alexandria, Cyprus, and Persia. The East, in the broadest sense of the word, was the major source of supply for valuable stuffs. In this sense the East ranges from China, famous for its silks, to Egypt and Constantinople. It was in Egypt and Constantinople that the Hellenistic and Eastern cultures were upheld—though in very different ways—through the intermediary of the art of the Copts and of Asia Minor, respectively, later receiving new impetus from Persia and Islam.

The fabrics mentioned in the *Liber Pontificalis* were used as altar frontals and altar cloths or as curtains *(vela)* for separating the presbytery from the body of the church reserved for the laity. *Brandea* was the word for linen cloths used to wrap relics; these cloths in themselves were viewed as contact relics and esteemed almost as highly as the veritable remains of the saints. These latter were displayed on cushions *(plumaciae)* covered with precious stuffs. It was only at a late date that the *tunica* worn by the clergy for divine service became highly ornate.

Of the innumerable donations of fabrics listed in the early documents, one example must here suffice, that of Leo III (795–816) to the church of Saint Paul. The pontiff endowed the basilica with four *vela* of white silk adorned with roses *(alba oloserica rosata)*; one had in the center a cross and gamma-shaped symbols in gold braid. He also presented the church with nine curtains in Tyrian silk edged with gold.

The ornamental motifs on these fabrics were not always typically Christian. Indeed, the sixth-century Syrian pieces reproduced in plates 93 and 94 with representations of the Annunciation and the Nativity are extremely rare. As a rule, stuffs were chosen not for their theological statement but for the value set on them merely as fabrics. They were viewed as works of art, and therefore aesthetic considerations came before iconographic. This also explains how it was that typically secular fabrics were employed for sacred purposes (plates 91, 92, 95, 96, 97).

The lively trade in precious stuffs between the East and the West naturally encouraged the emigration of weavers and other textile workers from one trading center to another. These craftsmen brought with them the techniques and ornamental motifs in vogue in the places where they came from. For this reason it is sometimes extremely hard to determine the exact origin of a given fabric, particularly since stuffs often display considerable eclecticism in both manufacture and design.

*A.P.*

90 Persian silk fabric with cock in medallion ▷

91 Byzantine silk fabric with winged horses

92 Persian silk fabric with lions in medallion ▷

93 Syrian silk fabric with the Nativity in medallion

94 Syrian (?) silk fabric with the Annunciation in medallion

◁ 95 Byzantine silk fabric with hunting scenes in medallion

96 Byzantine (?) silk fabric with two lions and palm trees

# 9 Early Carved Ivories

◁ 97 Syrian (?) silk fabric with a man wrestling with a lion

Ivory, whether elephant, walrus, or hippopotamus, is a material particularly well suited for carving; in addition, it easily takes a high polish. These natural properties favor its use for plastic representations. In the more pictorial carvings, the smooth surface combines with the clear line of the design to produce both contrasted and finely graded transitions from light to shade. For this reason ivory can satisfy the most exacting demands and at the same time, being so easy to work, it should be ideal for folk art.

Because it is so costly and hard to come by, however, this material has never been adopted in popular handicrafts and has always been linked with an aristocratic art. As such, ivory has been used since remote antiquity and can be traced back to the Palaeolithic period. The "historical" origin of ivory carving is located in the Middle East. Hittite and Phoenician merchants were the first to bring ivory to Western markets.

At a very early date (between the eighth and the seventh century before Christ) there developed ivory-carving schools and workshops that had no connection with the East. We know how highly the Greeks prized ivory and with what refinement they worked it. As an extremely valuable material it was used side by side with gold in their statues, which for that reason were called *chryselephantine* (made of gold and ivory).

Another peak period for ivory carving was the heyday of the Byzantine culture toward the end of the Roman empire. The main centers were Syria, Alexandria, and especially Constantinople. An eloquent example of Alexandrine art is the pyxis reproduced in plates 98–101. The narrative vein and lively expression of the representation, which bear witness to the Hellenistic tradition, are overshadowed by the rhythmically abstract atmosphere that envelopes the figures, which seem almost to be engaged in a dance. In an original, typically Alexandrine fashion, the clearly drawn outlines, the supple forms, and the neat separation of figures and background unite in a harmonious whole the contributions of different cultures. The same characteristics, though in a less striking form, recur in the Triumph sculptured on Bishop Maximian's pulpit at Ravenna.

From Alexandria the classical heritage spread throughout Europe thanks chiefly to the monasteries (for example, the Abbey of Saint Gall in Switzerland). Those established by the Benedictine Order indeed often comprised workshops in the proper sense of the term. Ivory carving, like every true art—and unlike techniques that depend exclusively on the materials employed—developed in accordance with the prevailing culture and taste. This explains the introduction of barbarian forms and Islamic themes in the Rambona diptych (plates 103, 104).

Diptychs offered a vast field for ivory carving, particularly during the Byzantine period when sculpture in stone experienced a long decline. It became the custom to present important personages on solemn occasions with two small tablets joined together with hinges so that they opened and closed like a book. The inner surfaces of the tablets were coated with wax, which made them suitable for a written message; their outer surfaces were tastefully decorated, usually with portraits of public figures, symbols of rank, or emblems, the intention being to honor the recipient. These folding tablets or diptychs became extremely popular, especially after the fourth century. They were so highly considered that in the year 384 the emperor Theodosius issued an edict restricting their use to consuls. Constantinople, capital of the new empire, was the major center for their production and use.

The fashion for diptychs had two effects. The first, though less important, was that they led to a type of article which developed through many variants either into small altars (plates 113–115 and, for instance, the famous Harbaville Triptych now in the Louvre) or into the finely worked tablets in several jointed parts which continued to be produced right up to the Renaissance and even later. The second, more important, effect was that they formed objects which had the dual advantage of being very valuable and extremely handy. This gave rise to the idea of the "portable" work of art, which, like the diptychs and book covers, could at the same time be an item of practical use.

Ivory was not employed exclusively for religious articles and for that reason was not banned by the Iconoclasts of the eighth and ninth centuries, although they did restrict its use to purely ornamental, secular objects. During the Carolingian period ivory received, so to say, an outward confirmation of its inward nobility. Creative workshops were established, particularly on the lower and middle Rhine and also on the Moselle. Besides confirming the workability of ivory and its suitability for portable articles, the objects produced in these centers reflect an artistic sensibility characteristic of the time and the place. These miniatures reveal to best advantage the distinctive typology and the wealth of forms and images of the period.

This development was not restricted to one area or style, of course. The little tablet of unknown provenance illustrated in plate 105, for instance, clearly derives from Byzantine book illumination, which was the major source of inspiration for the production of ivory objects in the Slavonic countries. Another example of this influence is the Lorsch book cover (plates 106–110) which, though apparently carved on the island of Reichenau in Lake Constance, displays Hellenistic and Byzantine types and motifs.

With the disintegration of the Carolingian empire, the art of ivory carving in France went from bad to worse. In Germany, on the contrary, it experienced a second heyday under the Ottonian dynasty, though of a totally different character. Through the intermediary of the monasteries, ivory carvers returned to the West; but this time, far from the influence of the more abstract Byzantine style, they followed a markedly naturalistic trend. By degrees there prevailed the artistic sensibility and attitude that characterized the onset of the Romanesque style and led to the conceptions of what is called the medieval renaissance.

The easy workability of the medium, which in art is synonymous with freedom and therefore with stylistic perfection, and the transportability of objects carved in ivory, which made those works suitable for gifts well calculated to express the rank of both the donor and the recipient—these two characteristics make ivory carving an authentic witness of various cultural epochs.

*A.P.*

98–101 Ivory pyxis with scenes of Christ's miracles

◁ 102 Ivory diptych with birds in grapevines

103 Ivory diptych from Rambona Convent

104 Detail of the Rambona diptych (plate 103): The Virgin and Child Enthroned

105 Ivory book cover: The Nativity ▷

Η ΓΕΝΝΗϹΙϹ

106 and 107
Paneled ivory book cover, with and without its gilt frame from Lorsch, Germany

108–110 Details from the Lorsch book cover (plate 106)

111 Ivory book cover: Christ in Glory Between Angels and Saints

112 Detail of ivory book cover (plate 111) ▷

EGO
SIRE
SURREC
CIOET
UITA

◁ 113 Detail of the central inner panel of the Byzantine triptych (plate 115): Christ Enthroned

114 Outer panels of the large Byzantine triptych in ivory

115 Inner panels of the large Byzantine triptych in ivory

116
The Byzantine triptych, closed

117
Detail from the outer right wing of the Byzantine triptych ▷

118 Detail from the outer central panel of the Byzantine triptych ▷

119 Painted ivory Crucifixion panel

# 10 Icons and Crosses

Domestic worship and private piety encouraged the production of small, handy devotional objects, for which it was quite natural to employ precious materials: gems on which religious motifs were carved, small bejeweled icons, gold pectoral crosses.

The plain cross was commonly used as a devotional object at a very early date, but the crucifix—the image of Christ crucified—first appears much later. The reason is that it evoked all too crudely the manner in which criminals were put to death. Christian writers like Minucius Felix, who lived in the third century, were well aware of this and did not scruple to point out that devotion to the crucifix laid Christians open to ridicule. Proof of this is the cross painted on the wall of the Paedagogium on the Palatine in Rome: the crucified Christ is portrayed with an ass's head and beneath is the inscription: "Alexamenos worships his god."

If the crucifix is meant to recall the historic moment of Christ's martyrdom on Golgotha, the cross without a body symbolizes rather the instrument of Redemption, the pillory that became the token of victory, a token well calculated to be the spiritual symbol of a concrete event.

Constantine combined the cross with the phrase *In hoc signo vinces* (In this sign shalt thou conquer). His mother Helena discovered the "true Cross," fragments of which were later distributed throughout the world. The cross became an object of devotion. It no longer served chiefly as a memento of the Passion but was prized as the symbol of victory over evil, the emblem of triumph. That is how writers and Fathers of the Church celebrated and extolled it. Lactantius at the turn of the third century called the cross "emblem of the Lord, heavenly emblem" *(signum domini, signum caeleste)*. He was followed in his interpretation by Prudentius (second half of the fourth century), Sedulius (fifth century), and Venantius Fortunatus, who died in 605 as bishop of Poitiers and was the author of two famous hymns—*Pange lingua gloriosi* and *Vexilla regis prodeunt*.

The cross came to be the tangible expression of the essential statement of Christianity, the doctrine of Redemption. In course of time it was attributed with the power to banish evil and give health. As symbol of the Christian hope of salvation it found a multitude of uses: it was planted on graves, worn around the neck, placed in the hands of the dead. The cross became a religious commodity. There are innumerable precious specimens, of which only two can be mentioned here: the cross of San Lorenzo fuori le Mura in Rome (plate 127), inscribed with passages from the Gospels that refer to the Saviour, and the large cross for "the mortal sleep of Olympius" (plate 128). There were also devotional crosses in the proper sense of the term, designed for sewing on people's clothes and not for public use. Though they were more personal in character, these gold crosses were worn as badges of honor.

Small cruciform boxes worn around the neck or on the breast often served as containers for relics, whose presence naturally much enhanced their devotional value. Such precious pectoral crosses and pectoral reliquaries were adorned with portrayals of Christ or other holy persons (plates 132–133).

The evolution of the crucifix merits a few remarks. The wooden doors of Santa Sabina in Rome, which date from the fifth century, are probably the earliest evidence that the representation of Christ crucified was no longer the problem it once had been. In the Crucifixion panel, the cross all but disappears behind the outstretched arms of the naked Christ (the same applies to the crosses of the two thieves). Only a little later, on an ivory carving now in the British Museum, the cross is already clear to see behind Christ's body. These crucifixes are followed by a great many of Byzantine origin, for example, those in the Rabbula Gospel of 586, now in Florence, and in an early eighth-century fresco in Santa Maria Antiqua in the Roman Forum. In the fresco Christ wears a sleeveless tunic *(colobium)* and is portrayed as still alive, with open eyes and an apparently almost weightless body which has not succumbed to but triumphed over death. This is the first instance of the iconographic theme of *Christus triumphans* (plates 132, 134).

In later works we find Christ on the cross clothed only in a loincloth *(perizoma)*. Though the eyes are still wide open, the head begins to droop; the accent is placed on the Saviour, but the Saviour in the death throes. This marks the start of a new way of looking at the cross: people visualized the pain Christ suffered as a man. The process culminated in the *compassione* of Saint Francis of Assisi, who experienced all the pangs of Christ's Passion, beginning with His physical suffering.

During this period, artists endeavored to convey that suffering in all its poignancy, instead of glossing over it. Many of their works show the Saviour with swollen abdomen and caved-in chest, gasping for breath. He writhes in agony and gives up the ghost *(emisit spiritum)*. His head slumps down on His shoulder. His dead body hangs so heavy that the nails which hold Him to the cross are scarcely able to bear the weight. This trend is reflected in a hectic handling. There developed an expressionism which, particularly in the late Gothic period, led artists to identify themselves completely with the pain of crucifixion and feel themselves caught up in the tragedy of the Passion as followers in the footsteps of Christ. Though the feelings expressed were perfectly genuine, the art sometimes degenerated later into a formal play of lines that was beautiful but empty. In northern Europe, particularly in Germany, active absorption in Christ's death found outstanding adepts.

Christ is often represented as a king with a crown upon His head, in a certain sense as *Triumphator* (plates 136, 137). Wherever possible the body of the crucified Christ was decorated; the loincloth, for instance, was frequently gilded or enameled. But that did not lessen the emphasis on the drama which announced a new period in art history totally alien to the deeply rooted art of Byzantium. In the twelfth century the Rhenish-Westphalian School, with Roger von Helmarshausen in the lead, established the new iconographic style and, more important still, the new artistic language. *A.P.*

120 Mosaic portrait of Saint Theodore of Tyre

121 Relief portrait in steatite of Saint Theodore Stratelates in prayer

123 Relief in "pietra dura," obverse side showing the Archangel Gabriel

124 Relief in "pietra dura," reverse side showing the Virgin and Child

◁ 122 Relief portrait in steatite of Saint Pantaleimon

125 Relief in green jasper: Christ Enthroned

126 Relief in red jasper: Christ in a Mandorla

CRVX
MORSINIMICETIBI
ESTVITAMI

◁ 127 Gold reliquary cross

◁ 128 Bronze votive cross

◁ 129 Gold votive cross

◁ 130 Gold votive cross

131 Pectoral reliquary cross in gilded and enameled bronze

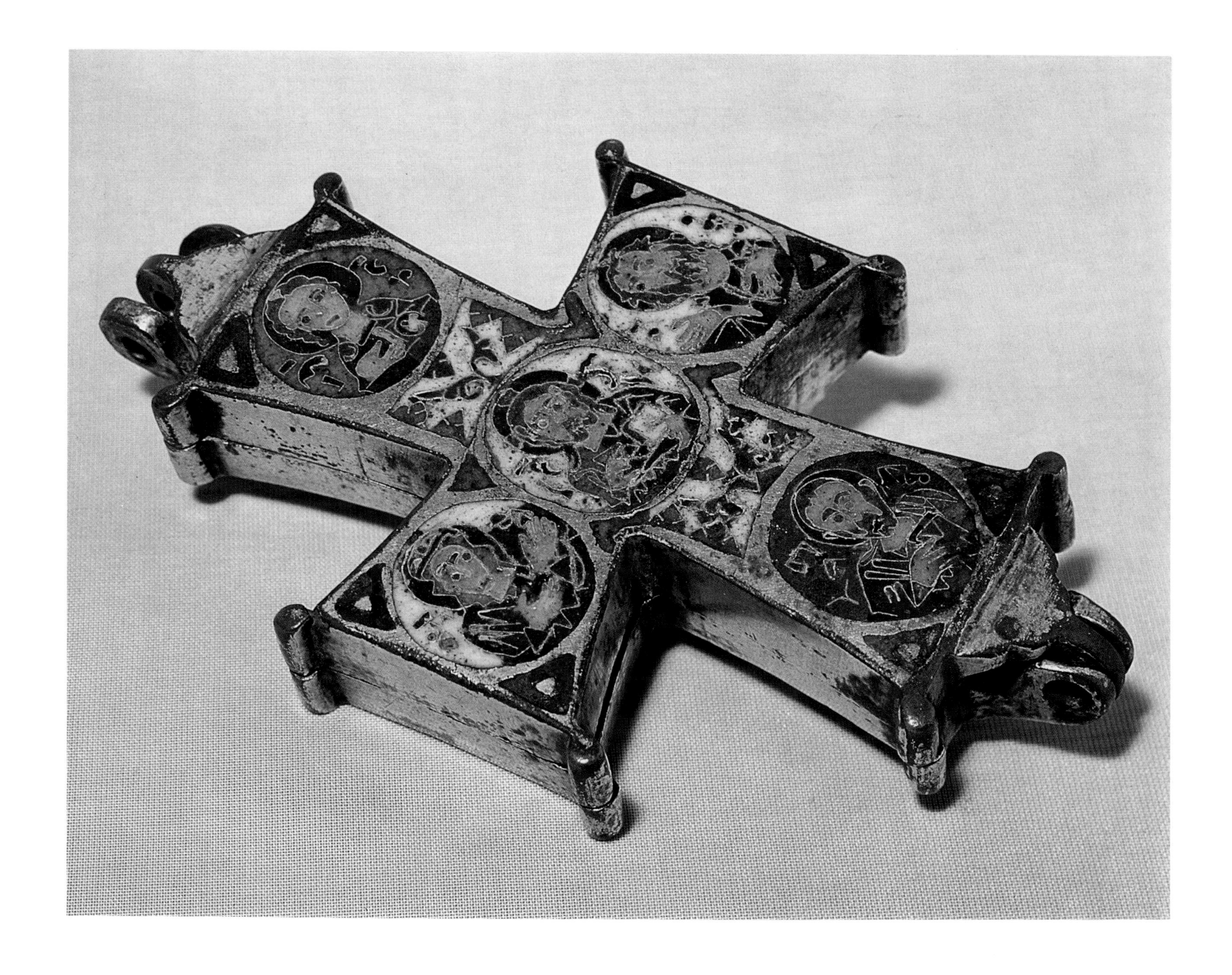

132–133 Pectoral reliquary cross in gilded bronze, obverse and reverse ▷

134 Gold pectoral cross ▷

135 Bronze pectoral cross molded in the shape of the crucified Christ ▷

◁ **136** Crucifix of gilded copper with champlevé enamel

◁ **137** Bronze crucifix

# 11 Enamelwork

The practice of melting together various sorts of sand was introduced at a very early date. This produced a paste which, when cold, took on brilliantly clear, wonderfully luminous colors. Enamel had been discovered. The colors were sometimes pure, sometimes blended in various ways. Much later the same paste, purified of the coloring matter, gave rise to the material we now call glass. Consequently glass is merely a subspecies or further development of enamel.

Enamel fulfills all the conditions needed to be considered one of the most important raw materials for artistic production. Its colors are fascinating, it is easy to spread, and it offers vast scope for graded light effects. These are the most elementary requirements of the visual arts.

In works of this class the enameled areas are limited by visible ridges. Hence the colored element, the enamel in the narrow sense of the word, is always linked with a design, namely with an outer form that can be modified at will. So enamelwork combines all the elements of figurative representation. Just as the glassy paste can assume many, indeed innumerable different colors, so the design that encloses the colored areas admits of great variety. It can range from the predrawn outlines of human figures to the most abstract forms; it can also serve to heighten the effect in the midst of the colored mass.

This demonstrates what extraordinary complexity the notion of "enamelwork" involves. Scholars differ enormously in their opinions on the date, derivation, origin, and mutual influences of the various schools working in this medium, and on the invention and renovation of the technical processes. When examined in detail these factors are so difficult to reduce to a common denominator that it seems justified to restrict the analysis here to the essential features of the enameler's art. The basic schemas admit of such a variety of works that a certain number of distinctions must perforce be drawn.

Enamels are distinguished and designated first and foremost by the two major techniques used for their production. In the first process the paste is poured into cavities previously cut in a metal base. The metal provides a good support for the paste. This type of enamel is called champlevé; its characteristic feature is that the contour lines are not very clearly defined. They are obtained by modifying the metal support and therefore achieve a more plastic effect, or at least make the transitions seem less abrupt. The metal that remains visible may be an essential element of the image—the heads of the figures are often made of pure metal and stand out in relief against the enameled areas (plate 144)—or merely form a decorative pattern after the manner of *opus vermiculatum* (plate 143). In both cases the work is given a highly individual character by the blending of the various elements and the intrinsic value of each. The major details of the champlevé technique have been known from time immemorial.

The other technique first appears in the early Middle Ages and was in vogue up to the end of the Romanesque period. Extremely thin strips of metal (often less than a millimeter thick) are soldered onto a base, giving rise to cell-like spaces into which the molten mass of enamel is poured. This technique is called cloisonné and its properties and effects are diametrically opposed to those of the champlevé technique. The design is clear and precise and—this is most important—increases in density as the colors of the enameled areas increase in number. Design and color, linework and polychromy, mutually stress each other. If we imagine the base and the little strips to be made of gold, we can easily visualize the brilliant radiance of precious objects made by the cloisonné technique.

To understand the development and popularity of cloisonné enamels, we must call to mind Byzantine painting or the mosaics of what is called the Second Golden Age, namely the period between the tenth and the twelfth century. Such works combine strict linearity with wonderfully bright colors. The gestures that had started to become more animated freeze again in a tortured immobility. Cloisonné enamel satisfied the requirements and the sensibility of that period superlatively well, which explains its wide dissemination.

The process of pouring the paste into the previously prepared cells varied considerably. It ranged from a cold or almost cold method—the mass in solid or almost solid state was, so to say, set in the cells—to a method that might be termed integral. It consisted in filling the cells with the sand mixture and putting the whole object into a furnace.

The famous cross of Paschal I (817–24) decorated with scenes from Christ's childhood (plate 75) is one of the most outstanding examples of cloisonné work. Other incomparable specimens that deserve special mention are the altar of Volvinius in Sant'Ambrogio in Milan (ninth century) and the Pala d'Oro in San Marco in Venice (eleventh century).

The peculiar properties of enamel favor, as we have seen, a vast range of techniques. At the end of the Middle Ages some artists went so far as to eliminate the metal base altogether and let light stream through transparent enamel. Others poured the paste in layers onto a uniform base, producing a ground color that blended with the many-hued reflections of the overlying layers of enamel. In this process the cells often differed in depth, giving rise to a great variety of transparencies, reflections, and refractions.

During the Romanesque period in particular gold was replaced as the base metal by copper, which cost less. Only the upper edge of the strips was gilt. The Limoges School, which was the most famous of that age, distinguished itself particularly by introducing another new procedure. Before the enamel had solidified completely, it was smoothed over with a paintbrush or small scraper. This treatment, which recalls painting, expanded the colored areas, making the transition from one color to another seem gentler, the design looser, and the enamel less transparent. This innovation coincided with the end of the Byzantine artistic sensibility, which was particularly appreciative of brilliant, radiant light. Plates 138 to 142 illustrate the new technique, which later developed into the so-called "painted enamel" that was much used until well after the Renaissance.

The great Byzantine and Italian schools of the early Middle Ages were succeeded by German workshops, mostly connected with monasteries such as those at Regensburg, Bamberg, Essen, and Brunswick. Subsequently, the workshops in Lorraine, Hildesheim, Cologne, and Aachen became increasingly important, chiefly because they had access to base metals and adopted the technique employed at Limoges.

*A.P.*

138 Statuettes of Christ Enthroned and two Apostles in gilded and embossed copper with enamel and semiprecious stones ▷

139 Detail of an Apostle statuette from the Christ Enthroned group (plate 138) ▷

140
Two Apostles from the Christ Enthroned group (plate 138)

141
The crook of a bishop's crozier in engraved, gilded, and enameled copper, with the scene of the Annunciation ▷

◁ 142 The crook of a bishop's crozier in engraved, gilded, and enameled copper, with Saint Michael Killing the Dragon

143 Enamel on copper plaque, with Adam Rising from the Dead

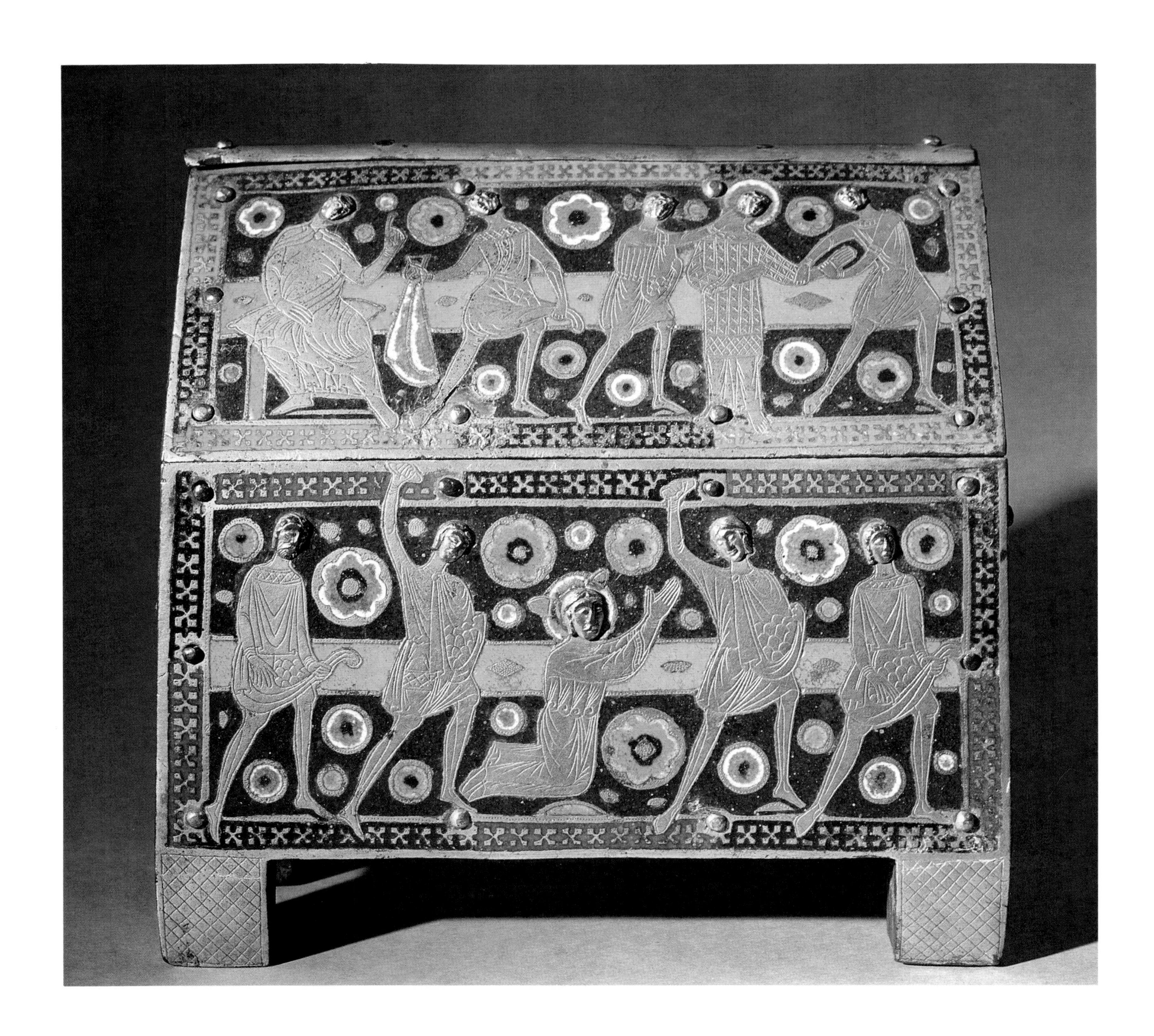

144 Casket for the relics of Saint Stephen, in engraved, gilded, and enameled copper over a wooden box

# 12 Gothic Ivories

The fourteenth century was the heyday of the style that is generally known as international Gothic. Europe seemed to be united in culture and artistic sensibility. The vast wave of the oriental style broke on encountering the fresh northerly breeze that preferred elegant design to mere colored light. The more attractive the design, the more it became an end in itself. But for all the energy and verve, a certain lightness still prevailed. Evidence of this artistic period is also found in the ivories it produced. But the mass of common or at least similar features frequently makes it difficult to judge or classify a work correctly.

For this reason each of the ivories reproduced here (plates 145, 147, 148) should preferably be viewed as a sample of the artistic trend that embraced the whole of Europe. Obviously, however, one must not overlook the fact that the Gothic style—especially in architecture and sculpture—was centered in France and Germany. Yet the source of Gothic painting must be sought in the art of the Sienese artist Simone Martini, which was later transplanted from Siena to the papal court at Avignon. As far as ivory carvings are concerned, the best Italian sculptors—the Tuscan School with Giovanni Pisano in the lead—found their models north of the Alps. An excellent example of Pisano's work in ivory is the small Madonna in the Treasure of Pisa Cathedral, a sculpture that reflects equally the strong personality of the artist and the influence of French culture and art.

Insofar as carving technique and artistic quality are concerned, Gothic ivories are in no way different from those of earlier times, except as regards isolated statuettes, which became more common, and a greater familiarity with statues of large size. The increase in technical refinement reveals a general cultural level that is typical of the art of the whole period.

A distinctive feature of ivory tablets (diptychs, book covers, and portable altars) is the architectural frame. Superimposed on the work independently of scenes and figures, it divides up the representation and gives it depth. In this way these ivory tablets acquire qualities similar to those of paintings. Clarity of design becomes less important, and the result is an atmosphere that unites and penetrates the various parts of a work in the aesthetic sense and also as regards the purely sensuous pleasure it gives.

When we examine the little tablets of plate 145, we feel as if we were looking at one of those magnificent stained-glass windows that bring to life not only the room they illuminate but also the images which adorn them. And if we consider that these ivories were originally painted over completely in bright hues, obliterating the color of the basic material, the comparison becomes more obvious still.

This is one more proof of the unity of culture, the harmony of opinion, and the concordance of taste which, though typical of every stylistic period, seem to have been particularly in evidence during the Gothic age.

*A.P.*

145 Ivory diptych with scenes of the Passion of Christ ▷

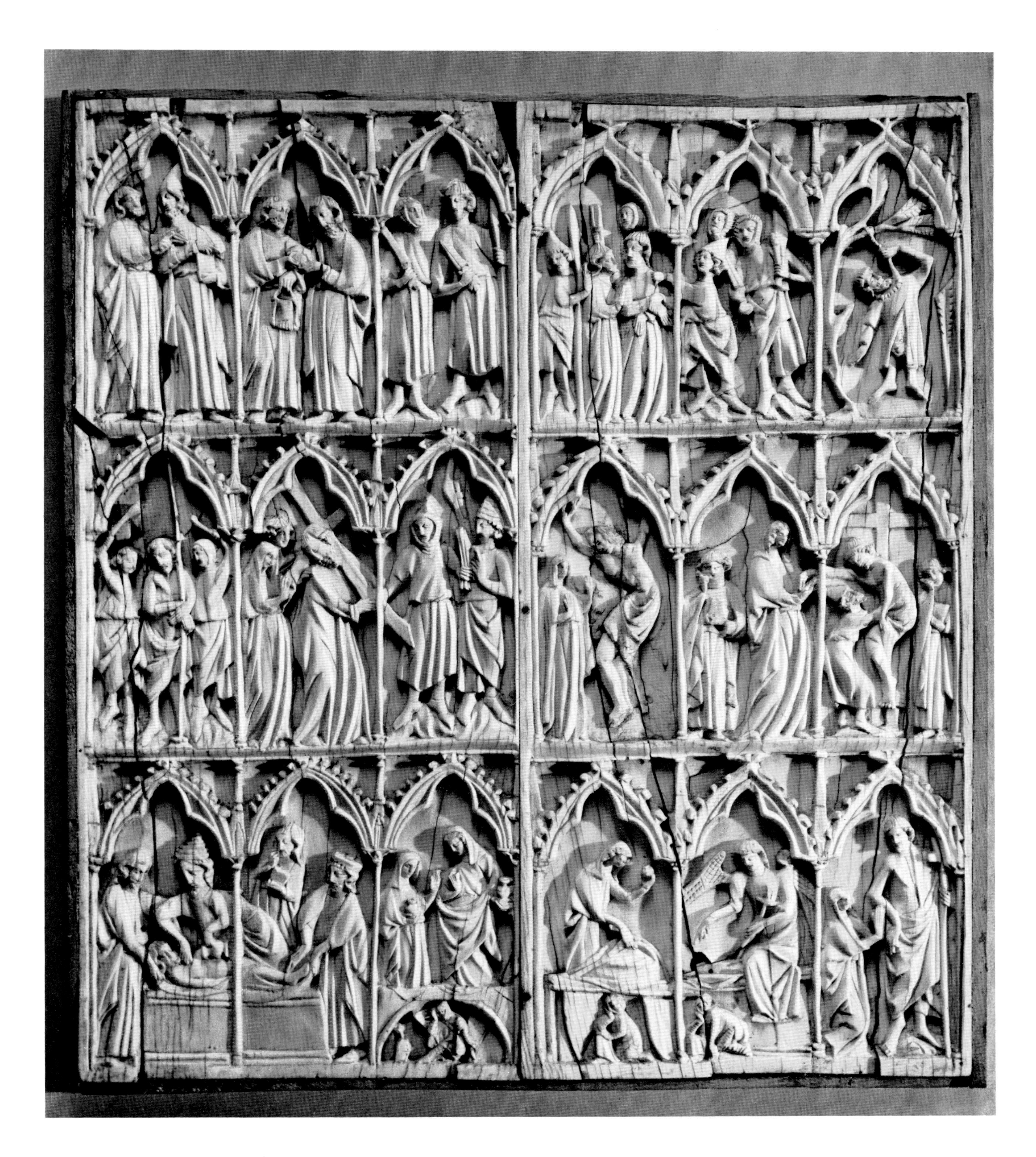

◁ 146
Ivory statuette: Virgin and Child

147
Ivory diptych with scenes from the life of Jesus and Mary

148 Ivory diptych with scenes from the life of Jesus and the Last Judgment

149 Three ivory mirror backs with secular scenes ▷

# Catalogue

1– 62: Georg Daltrop
63–149: Adriano Prandi

*1* View from the dome of Saint Peter's over the Belvedere Courtyard and the long wing that houses the Vatican Library's art collections.

*2 Greek votive relief: Horse and Rider.* Marble. 21 1/4 × 24 5/8″. About 400 B.C. Probably from Tyndaris, Sicily.

The bridle is missing; there is a hole in the horse's neck from which it may have been appended. The rider wears a cloak *(chlamys)* and a hat *(petasos)*. The horseman motif was popular in Greece during the classical period (cf. the Parthenon frieze, now in the British Museum).

Literature: P. Arndt and G. Lippold, in Brunn–Bruckmann, *Denkmäler griechischer und römischer Skulptur*, plate 729, right. Wolfgang Helbig, *Führer durch die öffentlichen Sammlungen klassischer Altertümer in Rom*, vol. 1, 4th ed. (Tübingen, 1963), p. 370, no. 471.

*3 Portrait head of the emperor Augustus.* Bronze. Height 15″ (lifesize). Probably cast in Rome during the reign of Augustus (27 B.C.–A.D. 14).

Portraits in bronze are not very common because the metal, easy to melt down, was in great demand later. This head is particularly valuable for its excellent quality.

Literature: B. Nogara, in *Römische Mitteilungen* 29 (1914): 186 ff., plates 11–13. Helbig, *Führer durch die öffentlichen Sammlungen klassischer Altertümer in Rom*, 1 (4th ed., 1963): 374 ff., no. 477.

*4 and 5 Two columns, each with a pair of Tetrarchs in relief.* Porphyry. Height of columns 12′ 7 1/2″; height of figures 22″. About A.D. 300. According to F. Albertini, from the vicinity of Aurelian's Temple to the Sun; first documented in Sixtus IV's chapel in Old Saint Peter's, which was consecrated in 1479; placed in the Vatican Library under Pius VI (1559–65).

The columns taper toward the top. The reliefs are carved at the upper end of the shaft; figures and shaft are in one piece. The original use of the columns is not known. Another specimen of portraits of Tetrarchs in porphyry can be seen outside Saint Mark's in Venice.

Literature: R. Delbrueck, *Antike Porphyrwerke* (Berlin, 1932), pp. 91 ff., plates 35–37. Helbig, *Führer durch die öffentlichen Sammlungen klassischer Altertümer in Rom*, 1 (4th ed., 1963): 369 ff., no. 470.

*6 Mithraic deity in human form with lion's head.* Marble. Height 60″ (including orb). Late 2nd century.

Much restored: the head, both arms with attributes, both wings, both legs below the knees, and the orb (probably completed on the basis of the statue reproduced in plate 7). For significance, see the commentary to plate 7. Interesting details are the signs of the zodiac in relief on the body.

*7 Mithraic deity in human form with lion's head.* Marble. Height 65″. Dated A.D. 190, by the inscription. From the Mithraeum at Ostia, discovered between 1794 and 1800.

A nude figure with lion's head and uraeus, the body encircled six times by the serpent's coils (symbolizing the spiraling path of the sun in the sky); only the stumps of the wings (symbols of the winds) are preserved; in each hand a key with twelve perforations (emblem of the power to open the gates of heaven); in the right hand a staff (the mark of royal authority); on the chest Jove's thunderbolt. On the base: Vulcan's hammer and tongs, the herald's staff of Mercury, the cock and pine cone of Aesculapius or Attis.

Inscription: C. VALERIUS HERACLES PAT[ER] ET C[AII] VALERII VITALIS ET NICOMES SACERDOTES S[UA] P[E]C[UNIA] P[O]S[UERUNT]. D[E]D[ICATUM] IDI[BUS] AUG[USTIS] IM[PERATORE] COM[MODO] VI ET SEPTIMIANO CO[N]S[ULIBUS].

Literature: *Corpus inscriptionum latinarum*, vol. 14, ed. H. Dressel (Berlin, 1899), pp. 65 ff. F. V. M. Cumont, *Textes et monuments figurés relatifs aux mystères de Mithras*, vol. 2 (Brussels, 1896), p. 117, no. 137, and p. 238, no. 80, fig. 68. G. Becatti, *I mitrei* (Rome, 1954), vol. 2 of *Scavi di Ostia*, p. 119, plate 36, 1. M. J. Vermaseren, *Corpus inscriptionum et monumentorum religionis Mithriacae*, vol. 1 (The Hague, 1956), p. 143, no. 312, fig. 85. F. V. M. Cumont, *Die orientalischen Religionen im römischen Heidentum*, 4th ed., reprint (Darmstadt, 1959), plate 1, 1.

*8–14 The Aldobrandini Wedding.* Mural painting in fresco: pigments mixed with lime wash, applied on fresh plaster. 36 1/4 × 95 1/4″. From the Augustan period about the date of Christ's birth. Found in 1604–5 on the Esquiline behind the church of San Gerolamo (since demolished), not far from the present-day Piazza Vittorio Emanuele.

In 1962 the fresco was stripped from the original wall in *opus reticulatum*, thoroughly cleaned, and freed from the overpainting applied during previous restorations. The entire upper part of the frame and two-thirds of the lower part on the left-hand side were done anew.

The explanation suggested here differs from those made previously in that it does not presume that the couch represents the bridal bed and therefore that the scene is set in the bridal chamber, pending the imminent arrival of the bridegroom. The identification of the youth at the head of the bed as the groomsman is based on a recent German edition of Catullus (O. Weinreich, *Catull: Liebesgedichte und sonstige Dichtungen, Lateinisch und deutsch* [Hamburg, 1960]), which reads lines 83–85 as:

*Wahre Scham lässt sie zögern noch,*
*als sie deutlicher jetzt* ihn *hört,*
*weint sie, weil sie soll folgen.*

Literature: For Catullus' sixty-first poem, a song for the wedding of Manlius Torquatus and Vinia Aurunculeia, see F. W. Cornish,

*The Poems of Gaius Valerius Catullus, Latin and English*, Loeb Classical Library, no. 6 (quoted in the text). For examples of wedding festivities, see W. Schadewaldt, *Sappho, Welt und Dichtung, Dasein in der Liebe* (Potsdam, 1950), pp. 32ff. Eighteenth- and nineteenth-century writers suggested that the fresco represents a mythical marriage, J. J. Winckelmann favoring that of Peleus and Thetis, E. Q. Visconti that of Dionysus and Ariadne, Eduard Gerhard that of Paris and Helen, and A. E. Braun that of Dionysus and Cora.

Fundamental and hitherto comprehensive publications: B. Nogara, *Le nozze Aldobrandine* . . . Collezioni archeologiche, artistiche e numismatiche dei Palazzi Apostolici, vol. 2 (Milan, 1907), pp. 1–35, plates 1–8. Nogara accepts the interpretation first suggested by C. Robert in *Hermes* 35 (1900): 685ff. and adopted by many authors (Amelung, Bulle, Pfuhl, Möbius, and Rizzo, for example) that the young man seated at the head of the bed is Hymenaeus; in his opinion, the marriage must not be viewed as mythological and the fresco was painted after a Greek model during the Augustan period. E. R. Curtius, "Zur Aldobrandinischen Hochzeit," in *Vermächtnis der antiken Kunst*, ed. R. Herbig (Heidelberg, 1950), pp. 119ff., sees the young man as a god—Dionysus waiting outside the chamber of his bride Basilinna; to him, the representation of the sacred marriage ceremony in the Anthesteria was a Roman copy of a late fourth-century Greek model. B. Andreae, in Helbig, *Führer durch die öffentlichen Sammlungen klassischer Altertümer in Rom*, 1 (4th ed., 1963): 360ff., no. 466, and in *Römische Quartalschrift* 57 (1962): 3ff., improves on Curtius in viewing the nuptials of the Greek deities as framed in a rigid Roman ceremonial. H. Marwitz, in *Antike und Abendland* 12 (1966): 97ff., plates 1–11, corrects the ancient painter (inadmissibly), keeps to Curtius' interpretation, and says that the model for the fresco was executed at Pergamum during the second century B.C.

15–21 *Picture frieze with scenes from the Odyssey*. Mural painted in fresco: pigments applied on fresh plaster. Height $45^5/_8$" throughout; width of sections varying from $57^1/_2$ to $60^5/_8$"; width of the architectural structure between the sections $12^5/_8$" (for reasons of space it has not been possible to reproduce all the sections on the same scale). Painted toward the end of the Roman republic, about 40 B.C. The first two sections were discovered by chance on April 7, 1848, during foundation work at no. 67–69 on the east side of the Via Graziosa (today Via Cavour) between Via Sforza and Via Quattro Cantoni. The rest of the cycle came to light during soundings on the adjoining plot. The city of Rome purchased the frescoes for 1500 scudi by a contract of June 22, 1850, and presented them to Pope Pius IX on January 2, 1851.

The frieze formed the upper part of a wall in *opus reticulatum* about 67 feet long (presumably a *cryptoporticus)*. The lower part of the wall has not been preserved. Immediately after their discovery the frescoes were removed by Succi. The first restoration and completion was carried out by Ettore Ciuli in 1852. In 1958–59 the two sections reproduced in plates 17 and 18, representing the destruction of the ships and the escape of Ulysses, were restored and the previous overpaintings and additions in tempera removed. The difference between these two sections and the others is clearly evident (compare, for instance, plates 16 and 17).

Literature: The standard publication with all information then available on the excavation and a report on literature previously published is Nogara's *Le nozze Aldobrandine, i paesaggi con scene dell'Odissea e altre pitture murale antiche conservate nella Biblioteca Vaticana e nei Musei Pontifici*, 2 (1907): 37–54, plates 9–32. Of recent publications the most stimulating and informative are: P. H. von Blanckenhagen, "The Odyssey Frieze," *Römische Mitteilungen* 70 (1963): 100–146, plates 44–53. Andreae, in Helbig, *Führer durch die öffentlichen Sammlungen klassischer Altertümer in Rom*, 1 (4th ed., 1963): 355ff., no. 465. A. Gallina, *Le pitture con paesaggi dell'Odissea dall'Esquilino*, Studi Miscellanei 6 (Rome, 1964).

22 *Inv. no. 230. Bell-shaped goblet with applied fish and shells (known as the Shell Goblet)*. Colorless glass, now very opaline; the fish and shells partly colored. Height $6^1/_8$"; diameter $5^1/_8$". About A.D. 300, presumably from a workshop in Cologne. Found in the Catacomb of Saint Callistus.

Recomposed from a great many fragments, but not complete; the base and the out-turned lip are missing. The modeled figures of fish and molluscs were blown separately, with anatomical details such as eyes and fins in different-colored glass attached afterwards. These figures are arranged rather irregularly in four rows on the surface of the goblet. The horn-shaped molluscs and some of the shells (not clearly visible in the reproduction) are adorned with glass-thread spirals. Underneath, remnants of three marine creatures (sea hedgehogs) that probably served as feet. Technically one of the finest specimens of ancient blown glass, although the execution is careless in parts. Closest parallels: Trevi, Landesmuseum G 694, and Cologne, Römisch-Germanisches Museum 63, 53.

Literature: A. Kisa, *Das Glas im Altertum* (Leipzig, 1908), p. 769, fig. 315. F. Dölger, *ΙΧΘΥΣ*, 4 (1927): plate 142, 1. F. Fremersdorf, *Die Denkmäler des römischen Köln*, vol. 6 (Cologne, 1961), pp. 27ff., plate 22.

23 *Fourteen small glass bottles: balsamaria, ampullae, bowls, and pitchers*. Blown glass. Most are colorless and covered with shimmering greenish or opalescent patina; others are blue, violet, or green. Heights varying from $1^1/_4$ to 7". Roman empire period (1st–3rd century). Those whose provenance is known were found in the Roman catacombs.

These are common specimens of utensils of daily use. Small tubular glass vessels made in two parts stuck together one above the other and fitted with two lugs (or a single tall handle) used to be termed no less generally than erroneously "tear bottles." Those with long neck and square belly are called Mercury bottles because some known specimens are adorned with the image of the god Mercury.

24 *Inv. no. 314. Fragment of a shallow bow with a Scene of the Glorification of Christ*. Cut glass, colorless. $6^3/_4 \times 4$". 4th century. From Ostia.

Two pieces that fit together have been preserved. There is a third fragment, in the same technique and with the same ornamental motif, that must have been part of the original bowl. It comprises the feet and pedestal of the saint incised on the side opposite the figure of Christ. The rim is neatly cut. The roundel is framed by three incised lines. In the center, Christ, bearded and haloed, in a long robe with sleeves. Between his head and hand, the monogram X P. At Christ's side and turned toward him, the figure of a saint also dressed in a long robe, but smaller in size. Behind him, a stylized palm tree. The entire picture represented Christ in Glory between two saints. The cut is vigorously modeled. Both the technique and the motif are typical of the fourth century.

Literature: G. B. de' Rossi, in *Bullettino di archeologia christiana* 6 (1868): 38, fig. 1. M. Floriani Squarciapino, in *Rendiconti della Pontificia Accademia Romana di Archeologia* 27 (1951–52): 257, fig. 2.

*25 Inv. no. 155. Small semispherical glass with fishing scenes.* Cut glass, colorless. Height 1$^5/_8$ to 1$^7/_8$″; diameter at tip 2$^5/_8$″. Early 4th century. Found in the catacombs.

The glass was broken and recomposed. The brim is cut and marked with two incised lines. In the figures only the main outlines and the major details of the inner drawing are cut; the remainder of the inner areas is merely ground. Neatly worked, the glass was probably executed in Rome during the reign of Constantine (306–37).

Literature: W. C. Hayes, in *American Journal of Archaeology* 32 (1928): 23 ff., plates 1 A and B.

*26 Seven phalerae: mask-shaped badges.* Chalcedony. Diameters varying from 1$^3/_8$ to 2$^1/_4$″. Roman empire period (1st–4th century). Where provenance is known, from the Roman catacombs.

Masks of uncertain significance (Medusa, Dionysus, Eros) carved on roundish stones. These latter are bored through—some both horizontally and vertically—presumably for fixing on a base. They are believed to be badges of some sort that could be attached to leather thongs and worn on the breast. These specimens are rather carelessly executed and have no great artistic value.

Literature: Adolf Furtwängler, *Die antiken Gemmen,* vol. 3 (Leipzig, 1900), p. 336. R. Righetti, *Opere di Glittica dei Musei Sacro e Profano,* Biblioteca Apostolica Vaticana, Museo Sacro, Guida 7 (Vatican City, 1955), p. 17, plate 6, 1–2. R. Righetti, in *Rendiconti della Pontificia Accademia Romana di Archeologia* 28 (1956): 330 and 334, plates 1, 4 and 7, 3–4. For other specimens, see F. Eichler and E. Kris, *Die Kameen im kunsthistorischen Museum* (Vienna, 1927), p. 88, nos. 105–109, plate 18.

*27 Inv. no. 427. Rectangular plaque with fish.* Cut rock crystal. 1$^3/_4$ × 4$^5/_8$″. Date and provenance unknown.

Mouth, eyes, fins, and tail are accurately reproduced. Suggestions concerning the original use (as for plate 28): window inset *(luminare)* or tomb identification mark.

Literature: F. Dölger, *ΙΧΘΥΣ,* 3 (1922): plate 95, 3. Righetti, *Opere di Glittica dei Musei Sacro e Profano,* Museo Sacro, Guida 7 (1955), p. 21, plate 10, 1. Righetti, in *Rend. Pont. Accad. Rom. di Arch.* 28 (1956): 331, plate 3, 3.

*28 Inv. no. 429. Rectangular plaque with goat under a tree.* Cut rock crystal. Traces of gold are still visible in the recesses of the boughs and leaves of the tree. 5$^1/_2$ × 3$^1/_4$″. Date and provenance unknown.

*29 Inv. no. 535. Fragment of cameo with head of the emperor Augustus.* Pale brown agate. 3$^1/_4$ × 3$^1/_8$″; thickness of rim $^1/_8$″; diameter when whole approximately 6″. Probably from the reign of Augustus (27 B.C.–A.D. 14). Found in the Catacomb of Saint Agnes in 1851.

The fragment is very carefully executed. Hair, cheek, eye, and part of forehead are still extant. The emperor wears the pointed crown. The head is framed by a wide rim; the reverse is hollowed out. Excellent workmanship: "It must have been a spectacular showpiece" (Furtwängler, *Die antiken Gemmen,* 3: 317, footnote 2). Righetti, *Opere di Glittica dei Musei Sacro e Profano,* Museo Sacro, Guida 7 (1955), p. 19, plate 9, 2. Righetti, in *Rend. Pont. Accad. Rom. di Arch.* 28 (1956): 316, plate 8, 4.

*30–51 Gold glasses: pictures in gold foil between colored bottom glass and colorless top glass.*

Basic publication: C. R. Morey, *The Gold-Glass Collection of the Vatican Library,* Catalogo del Museo Sacro della Biblioteca Apostolica Vaticana, vol. 4, ed. G. Ferrari (Vatican City, 1959). For the technique: A. Ilg, "Heraclius, von den Farben und Künsten der Römer," *Quellenschriften für Kunstgeschichte und Kunsttechnik des Mittelalters und der Renaissance* 4 (Vienna, 1873): 6 ff. The quotation is translated from Kisa, *Das Glas im Altertum* (1908), pp. 841 ff. Nothing else is known about the author Heraclius; the name is surely a pseudonym. Concerning the production of gold glass: T. E. Haevernick, in *Jahrbuch des Römisch-Germanischen Zentralmuseums, Mainz* 9 (1962): 58 ff.

*30 Inv. no. 788. Gold glass with full-length portrait of Dedalius surrounded by six scenes of carpenters at work in a shipyard.* Diameter 6$^1/_4$″. About A.D. 300. Found in the Catacomb of Saint Saturninus on the Via Salaria in 1731.

Recomposed from a great many fragments and mounted on a modern glass plate. The rim is broken off roughly all around. The surface is partly covered with an opalescent patina.

Dedalius wears breeches *(braccae)*, a belted, shirtlike robe *(tunica)*, and a cloak *(paludamentum)*. He has a T-square stuck in his belt, a roll of parchment *(rotulus)* in his left hand, and a staff with round knob *(baculum)* in his right hand. On each side are three carpenters at work. Those on the left are sawing, chopping a piece of wood, and drilling (with a bow drill). Upper right, Athena leaning on her shield and wearing the aegis with the Gorgoneion (a scaly shawl with the Medusa's head), which is her distinguishing attribute; she stands with raised right arm beside a carpenter who is making great play with hammer and chisel. Lower down a man is planing, and at the bottom a bearded bald-head is working on the bow of a boat.

The inscription: DEDALI ISPES TUA PIE ZESES Dedalius is the cognomen of the man portrayed in the center *(ispes = spes;* Dedalius, thy hope, drink, mayst thou live).

Literature: Morey, *Gold-Glass Collection*, p. 23, no. 96, plate 16. *Corpus inscriptionum latinarum*, 14: 2, no 7025.

*31 Inv. no. 731. Gold glass with galloping ass.* Diameter 3 3/4". 3rd century. Found in the Catacomb of Pontianus on the Via Portuense in November 1688.

Jagged edge all around; gold foil shows several rents; glass relatively thick and heavy, convex in front and correspondingly concave at rear. Inscription reversed right-to-left (apparently correct as reproduced here): ASINUS.

Literature: Morey, *Gold-Glass Collection*, p. 9, no. 34, plate 6.

*32 Inv. no. 733. Gold glass with Jewish religious objects and two lions.* Diameter 4 3/8". 4th century.

Jagged edge all around. Front slightly concave, rear correspondingly convex. Relatively thick, greenish, transparent glass. The roundel is divided horizontally and framed by a ring of dots alternately blue and red (now hard to distinguish). Above, a Torah shrine (with scrolls) flanked by lions. Below, two seven-branched candelabra and other ritual objects. Inscription: ANASTASI PIE ZESES.

Literature: Morey, *Gold-Glass Collection*, p. 27, no. 114, plate 19.

*33 Inv. no. 700. Gold-glass medallion with portrait of Eusebius.* Diameter 1 7/8". About A.D. 240. Found in the Catacomb of Saint Callistus in 1878.

Medallion framed by a circular band. Bottom glass deep blue. Portrait of a serious man with intense gaze and energetic expression. Bust dressed in *tunica* and *paludamentum*, held by a cross fibula. Excellent quality. Inscription: EUSEBI ANIMA DULCIS.

Literature: Morey, *Gold-Glass Collection*, p. 3, no. 3, plate 1. C. Albizzati, in *Römische Mitteilungen* 29 (1914): 242 ff., fig. 1 and plate 15, 1. H. von Heintze, in *Festschrift für E. von Mercklin*, p. 48, plate 26, 1.

*34 Inv. no. 639. Gold-glass medallion with portrait busts of a man and a woman.* Traces of patina in the center. Diameter 2 3/8". About A.D. 260. Found in the Catacomb of Pamphilus in 1920 let into the seal of a wall tomb.

The woman wears a mantle *(palla)*, the man a *tunica* and *paludamentum*. Their faces and hair styles recall, as closest parallels, those of the emperor Gallienus (253–68) and his wife, Salonia. Inscription: GREGORI SIMPLICI CONSECESCATES (not yet interpreted).

Literature: For the site of the find, see E. Josi, in *Rivista di archeologia cristiana* 1 (1924): 70, fig. 20. Morey, *Gold-Glass Collection*, p. 4, no. 7, plate 1.

*35 Inv. no. 701. Gold-glass medallion with family portrait: busts of a married couple and their son.* Diameter 1 3/4". About 480. From a Roman catacomb.

The medallion is framed by a circular rim. The woman wears *tunica* and *palla* draped across her breast; the man *tunica* and folded toga *(toga contabulata);* the son a little cloak buttoned on the right shoulder. Faces and hair styles recall, as most closely dated parallels, portraits of the soldier emperors Aurelian (270–75) and Probus (276–82) and Aurelian's wife, Severina.

Literature: Morey, *Gold-Glass Collection*, pp. 3 ff., no. 5, plate 1. Albizzati, in *Römische Mitteilungen* 29: 254 ff., fig. 4 and plate 15, 2.

*36 Inv. no. 699. Gold-glass medallion with portrait bust of a boy.* Diameter 1 5/8". Late 3rd century.

The medallion is framed by a plain circular border. Clothed bust of a child with headband. Inscription: SIMPLICI DULCIS.

Literature: Morey, *Gold-Glass Collection*, p. 4, no. 6, plate 1.

*37 Inv. no. 743. Gold glass with portrait busts of a man and a woman.* Diameter 4 1/4". About A.D. 230. Found in the Catacomb of Pamphilus on May 31, 1926, let into the front slab of a wall tomb.

Jagged edge all around. Medallion framed by a circular band. At the bottom, a sort of parapet. The figures wear tunic and cloak; the woman's cloak is knotted at her breast; the man's right arm is wrapped in his cloak so that only the hand is visible (after the Greek fashion). Inscription: GREGO RIBIBET PROPINA TUIS (presumably, *Gregori bibe et propina tuis* = Gregory, drink and drink to thine).

Literature: Morey, *Gold-Glass Collection*, p. 3, no. 1, plate 1. G. B. Ladner, *Die Papstbildnisse des Altertums und des Mittelalters*, vol. 1 (Vatican City, 1941), p. 20, fig. 6.

*38 Inv. no. 623. Gold glass embedded in a piece of roughcast: Nereid on a fabulous beast.* Diameter 5". 4th century.

Example of original use for wall decoration. Circular-band border. The Nereid is mounted on a fabulous beast with the front part of a stag and a marine monster's tail. Underneath it, a fish. The sea is indicated by dabs of blue pigment.

Literature: Morey, *Gold-Glass Collection*, pp. 24–25, no. 103, plate 17.

*39 Inv. no. 734. Gold glass with hunting scene.* Diameter 3 1/2". 4th century.

Jagged edge all around. Scene enclosed in a circular-band border. The hunter with outstretched arm urges his hounds at a stag; higher up, a doe with spotted coat. Trees indicate the landscape.

Literature: Morey, *Gold-Glass Collection*, p. 9, no. 35, plate 6.

*40 Inv. no. 777. Gold glass with the Raising of Lazarus and the Miracle at Cana.* Diameter 3 1/2". 4th century. From the Chigi Collection, 1756.

Jagged edge all around. Front concave. The medallion has a circular-band border and is divided horizontally into two parts. Above, the Raising of Lazarus; below, the Miracle at Cana. In both Christ holds a rod. Leaves are scattered over the whole picture to fill empty spaces.

Literature: Morey, *Gold-Glass Collection*, p. 26, no. 108, plate 18.

*41 Inv. no. 779. Gold glass with seven busts in roundels and one full-length figure.* Diameter 4 1/8". 4th–5th century.

Broken in several pieces and mounted on modern glass base. Jagged edge all around. Beardless busts flanked by scrolls *(rotuli)*.

Literature: Morey, *Gold-Glass Collection*, p. 25, no. 104, plate 18.

*42 Inv. no. 766. Gold glass with Christ's monogram and wreath between two young men, Laurentius and Cripranus (= Cyprianus).* Diameter $3^7/_8$". 4th century. From the Chigi Collection, 1756.

Framed by two circular bands with the inscription: HILARIS VIVAS CUM TUIS FELICITER SEMPER REFRIGERIS IN PACE DEI. Alongside the two young men, who are dressed in tunic and cloak and carry scrolls, the inscriptions LAURENTIUS and CRIPRANUS. Between them, Christ's monogram; above it, a wreath of leaves.

Literature: Morey, *Gold-Glass Collection*, p. 10, no. 36, plate 6.

*43 Inv. no. 705. Gold glass with the Raising of Lazarus.* Diameter $3^7/_8$". 4th century. From the Catacomb of Saturninus.

Jagged edge all around. The shroud-encased body of Lazarus in silver foil with the head in gold foil. Inscription: ZESUS CRISTUS.

Literature: Morey, *Gold-Glass Collection*, p. 9, no. 31, plate 5.

*44 Inv. no. 714. Gold glass with Jonah Resting Under the Gourd.* Diameter $4^3/_8$". 4th century.

Jagged edge all around. For another image of Jonah, see the lamp in plate 54.

Literature: Morey, *Gold-Glass Collection*, p. 12, no. 46, plate 7.

*45 Inv. no. 798. Gold glass with busts of Saints Peter and Paul in a square frame.* Diameter $3^1/_2$". 4th century.

The glass is broken in a circle all around. Inscription: PETRUS RAULUS (= Paulus; the substitution of R for P occurs frequently).

Literature: Morey, *Gold-Glass Collection*, p. 15, no. 60, plate 10.

*46 Inv. no. 721. Gold glass with bust of Saint Paul in a roundel.* Diameter $2^1/_8$". 4th century.

Inscription: PAULUS.

Literature: Morey, *Gold-Glass Collection*, pp. 14–15, no. 54, plate 9.

*47 Inv. no. 768. Gold glass with busts of Saints Peter and Paul and a crown of oak leaves.* Diameter $3^1/_2$". 4th century.

The heads of the two apostles are depicted in profile facing each other. Their types recall the portraits of the emperor Julian the Apostate (361–63) on coins. Inscription: PETRUS PAULUS.

Literature: Morey, *Gold-Glass Collection*, pp. 16–17, no. 67, plate 11.

*48 Inv. no. 634. Gold glass with the figures of Saints Peter and Paul.* Diameter $4^1/_8$". 4th–5th century.

The two figures, dressed in tunic and cloak, are depicted frontally side by side and identified by the inscription. Inside the circular-band border hang six garlands. Execution and quality are not good.

Literature: Morey, *Gold-Glass Collection*, p. 14, no. 56, plate 9.

*49 Seventeen small gold glasses with scenes from the Old and New Testaments.* Diameters varying from $^7/_8$ to $1^1/_2$". 4th century. From Roman catacombs.

Old Testament scenes: Tree of Knowledge with serpent; Adam; Tobias (with a fish in his right hand); Noah in the Ark; Moses striking water from the rock; one of the young men in the fiery furnace (with Persian cap and trousers, in an attitude of prayer; below, the symbol of fire); Daniel (with a round loaf).

New Testament scenes: Lazarus in the tomb; Christ bringing Lazarus back to life; Christ with the wine pitchers at Cana; a man carrying a bed (the healing of the lame man); a kneeling woman with outstretched arms; Christ with raised rod; Saint Peter.

*50 Eight gold glasses with figurative motifs.* Human figures; animals (dove of peace); Jewish ritual objects (shofar, a ram's horn blown on Yom Kippur, the Day of Atonement. Diameters varying from $^7/_8$ to $1^3/_8$". From Roman catacombs.

*51 Inv. no. 774: Gold glass with Saint Agnes as orant. Inv. no. 751: Gold glass with Saint Peter as the Moses of the New Covenant Striking Water from a Rock.* The water is represented by green pigment. Diameters $3^1/_4$ and $3^1/_2$".

Literature: Morey, *Gold-Glass Collection*, p. 20, nos. 82 and 81, plates 14 and 13. For the orant (a figure, usually female, in ancient art standing in an attitude of prayer, with outstretched arms), see T. Klauser, in *Jahrbuch für Antike und Christentum* 2 (1959): 133 ff.; more recently: 7 (1964): 67 ff.

*52 Inv. no. 924. Oil lamp with two spouts and suspension device.* Bronze, cast; ornamental plate soldered on handle. Height $7^7/_8$" (without chain), 20" (with chain). 4th century.

At the center of the container, a stylized leaf designed to function as funnel for pouring in the oil and as lug for the suspension chain. On the two channels leading to the spouts, two other lugs for suspension chains. As appendage to the handle, Christ's monogram (in Constantinian form) framed by a circle with eleven stylized palmettes.

*53 Inv. no. 1401. Oil lamp with the Good Shepherd from the workshop of Anni[us] Ser[apiodorus].* Terra-cotta. $4 \times 3^1/_4$". 3rd century.

Tip of spout and handle broken off. Shoulder decoration: alternately grapes and leaves. Stamped underneath.

Literature: W. F. Volbach, *Museo Sacro, Guida* (Vatican City, 1938), p. 10, fig. 3. For the Good Shepherd, see Klauser, in *Jahrbuch für Antike und Christentum* 1 (1958): 24 ff., fig. 4; more recently: 10 (1967): 82 ff.

*54 Inv. no. 1938. Oil lamp with Jonah Under the Gourd.* Terra-cotta. $4^1/_2 \times 3^3/_8$". 4th century.

Broken in several pieces and recomposed. The entire underpart is missing. Shoulder decoration: double circles. The same biblical motif as on the gold glass reproduced in plate 44. For representations of Jonah, see E. Stommel, in *Jahrbuch für Antike und Christentum* 1 (1958): 112 ff.

*55 Inv. no. 1380. Oil lamp with watcher's hut in vineyard.* Terra-cotta. $5^1/_8 \times 3^1/_8$". 4th century. From a Roman catacomb.

Part of the spout broken. Shoulder decoration: alternately heart-shaped leaves and circles. On the central disc: woven hut at the top of a leafless tree trunk. At the front edge of the hut floor sits a male figure playing a wind instrument. On the ground in front of him, a dog pursues a hare. On the other side of the hut, a bent figure gleaning. Explanation and interpretation after A. Stuiber, in *Jahrbuch für Antike und Christentum* 2 (1959): 86ff., fig. 10.

*56 Inv. no. 1381. Oil lamp with peacock.* Terra-cotta. $5^3/_4 \times 2^3/_4''$. 5th century.

Tip of spout broken off. Shoulder decoration: alternately triangles and rosettes.

*57 Inv. no. 933. Oil lamp with suspension device.* Bronze, cast and engraved. $4^1/_2$ (without chain) $\times 7^1/_8''$. 4th–5th century.

Filling-hole lid missing; hinge preserved. Shoulder decoration: engraved scrollwork. Handle appendage in the shape of a Latin cross with splayed ends and topped with a bird. Two lugs for fixing the suspension chains: on the cross, and between the filling hole and the wick hole.

*58 Inv. no. 867. Dish with wild boar hunt in roundel.* Silver, embossed, engraved, and stamped. Underside greatly oxidized (no stamp visible). Diameter $15^3/_8''$; diameter of roundel inside border $4^3/_4''$. 5th–6th century.

Literature: Volbach, *Museo Sacro, Guida* (1938), p. 11.

*59 (left) Inv. no. 861. Handled pitcher (amula) with medallions.* Silver, embossed and showing traces of gilding. Height $7^1/_4''$; diameter $2^1/_4''$. Early 5th century. Presumably from Rome.

Greatly oxidized. The foot restored and a small piece added under the lower handle insert. The body of the vessel is divided into seven zones by a cord motif. In the central zone, five medallions: Christ, Saint Peter, Saint Paul, and two other apostles. Above: a cross flanked by four doves; below: a lamb with four sheep.

Literature: H. H. Arnason, in *The Art Bulletin* 20 (1938): 225–226, fig. 35. Volbach, *Museo Sacro, Guida* (1938), p. 11, fig. 7. W. F. Volbach, *Frühchristliche Kunst* (Munich, 1958), p. 67, plate 121.

*59 (right) Inv. no. 858. Ampulla: small bottle with flattened circular body.* Silver, embossed (bronze foot and neck restored). Height (with foot and spout) $7^1/_4''$. 5th century.

The two flat sides of the circular body of the bottle have the same decoration: in the center, a medallion with an apostle (Saint Peter on one side, Saint Paul on the other) framed by two acanthus vines that grow up from below, interspersed with rosettes.

Literature: Arnason, in *The Art Bulletin* 20 (1938): 225–226, fig. 35. D. E. Strong, *Greek and Roman Silver Plate* (London, 1966), p. 192.

*60 and 61 Inv. no. 859. Small oval box with lid, decorated with figurative reliefs (capsella africana).* Silver, embossed and chased. $6^1/_4 \times 4 \times 3^1/_8''$. Early 5th century. From Henchir Zirara, southwest of Constantine, Algeria. Found in the altar of the basilica in 1884.

The bottom of the reliquary and the lower ornamental border are modern. On the lid (plate 61): Saint Polycarp with a martyr's crown between two tall candlesticks with lighted candles; above, the hand of God issuing from the clouds with a crown; below, the four rivers of Eden. On the side (plate 60): stag and hinds drink the waters of the four rivers; above them, Christ's monogram; right and left, a palm tree. On the side of the box not reproduced: the lamb of God with the cross on its back, with four sheep aproaching at right and left from Jerusalem and Bethlehem.

Literature: G. B. de' Rossi, in *Bullettino di archeologia cristiana* (1887), pp. 118ff., plates 8 and 9. G. B. de' Rossi, *La capsella argentea africana* (Rome, 1889). Arnason, in *The Art Bulletin* 20 (1938): 216, figs. 24 and 25. For the church in which the reliquary was found, see S. Gsell, *Les monuments antiques de l'Algérie* (Paris, 1901), p. 161; P. Wuilleumier, *Musée d'Alger*, Supplement, pp. 102–103.

*62 Inv. no. 864. Reliquary decorated with stylized palmettes and acanthus leaves.* Silver and niello. Height $7^1/_8''$; diameter $8^7/_8''$. 9th century. From the Santi Quattro Coronati.

The reliquary formerly contained the head of Saint Sebastian. Inside, a monogram which is believed to relate to Leo III (795–816). Around the foot, an engraved inscription with the name of Pope Gregory IV (827–44): AD DECORUM CAPITIS BEATI SEBASTIANI GREGORIUS IIII EPISCOPUS OBTULIT.

Literature: Volbach, *Museo Sacro, Guida* (1938), p. 11, fig. 8.

*63* The Sancta Sanctorum, the Papal Chapel in the Old Lateran Palace, now part of the building housing the Scala Santa.

Literature: The prime source is the *Liber Pontificalis*, ed. L. M. O. Duchesne (Paris, 1885–92). Another is the *Liber Censuum Romanae ecclesiae*, written in 1192 by Cencio Savelli, who later became Pope Honorius III (ed. Fabre-Duchesne, Paris, 1910; 2nd ed. 1952). In the fourteenth century the Treasure of the Sancta Sanctorum is mentioned in the *Ordines Romani* by Cardinal Gaetani (d. 1343); see N. Audrien, *Les Ordines Romani du haut moyen-âge* (Louvain, 1931–61). Basic publication: H. Grisar, *Die römische Kapelle Sancta Sanctorum und ihr Schatz. Meine Entdeckungen und Studien in der Palastkapelle der mittelalterlichen Päpste* (Freiburg im Breisgau, 1908). Recent literature: W. F. Volbach, *Il tesoro della Cappella Sancta Sanctorum*, Biblioteca Apostolica Vaticana, Museo Sacro, Guida 4 (Vatican City, 1941). T. Cempanari and T. Amodei, *La Scala Santa* (Rome, 1963).

*64 Inv. no. 1895. Lid of an ivory box with Christ Healing the Blind Boy.* Ivory. $4^3/_4 \times 2^1/_8''$. 5th–6th century. Egyptian workmanship. From the Sancta Sanctorum.

The considerable projection of the upper edge warrants the assumption that this was a sliding lid. Volbach suggests that it belonged to an oculist. The relief represents the miraculous healing of a boy who was born blind or lost his sight. In accordance with the Hellenistic style, Christ is depicted as beardless and clad in sleeved tunic and *pallium*. The boy, barefoot and dressed only in a tunic, stretches out his right hand in a tentative gesture; he holds a stick in his left hand. Jesus touches the boy's right eye with two fingers (presumably the sculptor aimed at rendering the spittle he used for the miracle). The left eye is already healed. A bearded figure, probably an Apostle or Isaiah, raises his right hand in a gesture of amazement.

The iconography is traditional. The closest parallels occur on sarcophagi with various scenes represented against an architectural background. The ivory relief is noteworthy for the firm delineation and the plastic rendering of the bodies. The style and composition indicate that it is probably a Coptic work.

Literature: P. Lauer, "Le Trésor du Sancta Sanctorum," *Monuments Piot* 15 (1906–7): 86–87. Volbach, *Il tesoro della Cappella Sancta Sanctorum*, Museo Sacro, Guida 4 (1941), p. 14. C. Cecchelli, *Vita di Roma nel Medio Evo* (Rome, 1951–60), 4: 232. W. F. Volbach, *Le arti minori in Vaticano*, ed. G. Fallani and M. Escobar (Florence, 1946), p. 602.

*65 Inv. no. 1911. Leaves of a diptych with portraits of Saints Peter and Paul.* Wax painting on wood panel. Each leaf 3³/₈ × 2¹/₄". 6th–7th century (Volbach); 2nd–3rd century, but also 4th–5th century, and "not later than the 4th century" (Cecchelli); "*ante* 816," but in the manner of an early Christian work (Ragghianti). From the Sancta Sanctorum.

The original hinge is missing. The two apostles are represented in the traditional manner (Peter with short beard and two rows of curly locks, Paul with pointed beard and balding forehead); they are dressed in tunic and *pallium* with the *clavi* and horizontal stripes. The drapery stresses the sculptural handling of the two three-quarter busts. The colors are rather dull but well matched, harmonizing perfectly with the gold ground. Pictures of Peter and Paul existed as early as the time of Eusebius (c. 265–340); see *Hist. Eccl.*, VII, 18,4, ed. Del Ton (Rome, 1964), p. 570. But these are particularly valuable because "*ab antiquo*" (Cecchelli, p. 643) they were held to be true likenesses of the apostles. Until the Renaissance that of Saint Peter was considered "*effigies vera et naturalis simillima*" (L. Bonincontri, *Cronicon sive Annales ab a. 903 ad a. 1458)*. On those grounds the diptych deserved a place among the relics of the Sancta Sanctorum and was probably carried in processions. A legend was spun around the likeness: according to a story that was widespread during the Middle Ages and was even depicted in the ancient atrium of the Vatican Basilica, in the portrait of Saint Peter the emperor Constantine recognized the apostle as he had seen him in a dream.

Stylistically, the work shows little or no direct Byzantine influence and is therefore probably of Roman origin. So on the whole Volbach, who views the diptych as a work of the Roman school, is substantially in agreement with Ragghianti, who sees it as a Roman copy of an early Christian original, even though the former attributes it to the seventh century, the latter to the ninth. And the apparent contradictions in Cecchelli's opinion—he also advanced the hypothesis that it might be a copy after a lost original—are easy to understand.

Literature: Lauer, "Le Trésor du Sancta Sanctorum," *Monuments Piot* 15 (1906–7): 20. Cecchelli, *Vita di Roma nel Medio Evo* (1951–60), 9–10: 634. C. L. Ragghianti, *L'arte in Italia*, vol. 2 (Rome, 1968), col. 512.

*66 and 67 Inv. no. 1883 a–b. Small wooden box with mementos from the Holy Land.* Painting in tempera inside the lid. 9¹/₂ × 7¹/₄ × 1⁵/₈". 9th century (Grisar); 10th–11th century (Lauer, Diehl); 6th century (Morey); 8th–9th century (Volbach); 7th–8th century (Cecchelli). From the Sancta Sanctorum.

The box still contains stones and bits of wood from the Holy Places; each specimen bears the indication of its provenance. The inside of the sliding lid, which still functions, is adorned with scenes from the life of Jesus. Below, the Nativity and Baptism; in the middle, the Crucifixion; above, the Holy Women and the Angel at the Tomb and the Ascension. On the outside of the lid, on a light-colored ground, the mandorla with Christ's monogram; on the sides, the name of Jesus in abbreviated form.

The box reflects the important part pilgrimages to the Holy Land played in the early Middle Ages. The scene of the Women at the Tomb is particularly significant because it seems to be the truest picture still extant of the Holy Sepulcher with its iron gates, the gravestone (marked with a cross), and the great rotunda of the Anastasis erected by Constantine and destroyed by the Persians under Khoraus II in 614. It was that date which led Morey to attribute the painting to the sixth century; he saw a confirmation of this in the parallels to the scene of the Crucifixion in the Syriacus Gospel Book written by Rabbula in 586. Actually, however, a direct comparison between the two scenes shows up their differences. The box should be given a later date. It may be a ninth-century copy executed in the East after a sixth-century model.

Literature: Lauer, "Le Trésor du Sancta Sanctorum," *Monuments Piot* 15 (1906–7): 97. C. R. Morey, "The Painted Panel from the Sancta Sanctorum," in *Festschrift zum 60. Geburtstag von Paul Clemen* (Düsseldorf, 1926), p. 151. Volbach, *Il tesoro della Capella Sancta Sanctorum*, Museo Sacro, Guida 4 (1941), p. 20. Cecchelli, *Vita di Roma nel Medio Evo* (1951–60), 9–10: 644.

*68 and 69 Inv. no. 1039. Small oval box with embossed reliefs.* Silver. 7¹/₂ × 4 × 2³/₄". 5th century (Cecchelli); 6th century (Volbach). From the Sancta Sanctorum.

On the lid, the Triumph of the Cross, embossed in imitation of a cross set with gems; below, two angels in adoration; upper left, the hand of God the Father issuing from the starry sky; upper right, the dove with a crown. This leads to the conclusion that the box was used as a reliquary of the True Cross. But the symbols allude to the Trinity, which makes this specimen extremely rare. On the sides, medallions with Christ and saints between stylized palm trees; above and below, ornamental bands in the shape of twisted cords. The execution, if not the design, bears the imprint of the West, but there is no evidence to show whether this is a Roman or an Eastern work.

Literature: H. Grisar, *Il "Sancta Sanctorum" ed il suo tesoro* (Rome, 1907), p. 84. Volbach, *Il tesoro della Cappella Sancta Sanctorum,* Museo Sacro, Guida 4 (1941), p. 15. Cecchelli, *Vita di Roma nel Medio Evo* (1951–60), 1: 20, 2: 700.

*70 Inv. no. 985. Casket and cushion for a reliquary cross.* Left, cushion that protected a lost gemmed cross containing a relic of the True Cross. Right, silver box for holding cross and cushion. From the Sancta Sanctorum.

The fabric, which may well be as old as the casket, is attributed by Volbach to the eighth century or the early ninth; Cecchelli dates it, with a question mark, to the seventh or eighth. The cushion itself may have been made up at the same time as the box (under Pope Paschal I, 817–24) or earlier.

The gemmed cross with its cushion (not necessarily the one still extant) is probably that which Pope Sergius I (687–701) found in the *sacrarium* of the basilica of Saint Peter: *Plumacium ex holosirico superpositum, quod stauracin dicitur invenit . . . crucem diversis ac pretiosis lapidibus perornatam" (Liber Pontificalis*, ed. Duchesne, p. 374). Some scholars view it as the cross presented to Pope Adrian I (772–95) by Charlemagne.

The cushion filled with wadding and covered with richly patterned linen is made up of seven pieces of cloth sewn together. It is in bad condition because the reliquary it supported was frequently anointed with oil: on special occasions, such as the Feast of the Elevation of the Cross, it was honored, anointed, and kissed. From the pattern and weave of the cloth, Volbach infers that the cushion is Byzantine; the choice of the ornamental motifs points to Alexandrian influences, while their constant repetition is a Persian (Sassanid) characteristic.

Literature: Grisar, *Il "Sancta Sanctorum" ed il suo tesoro* (1907), p. 182. W. F. Volbach, *La Croce: Lo sviluppo nell'oreficeria sacra,* Biblioteca Apostolica Vaticana, Museo Sacro, Guida 2 (Vatican City, 1938), p. 5. W. F. Volbach, *Stoffe Medioevali,* Biblioteca Apostolica Vaticana, Museo Sacro, Guida 6 (Vatican City, 1943), pp. 14, 45. Cecchelli, *Vita di Roma nel Medio Evo* (1951–60), 5–6: 290.

*71 Inv. no. 985. Casket for a reliquary cross (plate 70).* Silver, embossed, chased, and gilded. 11 × 10 $^7/_8$ × 2 $^1/_2$″. Probably executed in a Roman workshop.

The container, which weighs over four pounds, has the shape of the cross it protected. On the lid, six scenes: in the middle, the institution of the Eucharist; above, Jesus flanked by the Evangelists; left, the Miracle at Cana; right, Jesus' farewell before the Ascension; below, Christ appears in the upper chamber. The central scene is framed by the inscription: PASCHALIS / EPISCOPUS / PLEBI DEI / FIERI IUSSIT. The lid is closed with movable rings and fixed hooks. It rests on a cordlike ridge. The handle was added later. On the twelve lateral panels are reproduced twelve scenes from the life of Christ after the Resurrection. Only the raised parts of the relief are gilded. The Virgin Mary is present in each of the scenes on the lid.

The execution is homogeneous, yet the work of assistants can be recognized in various parts: in the scene of the Ascension, for example, only the figures in the foreground show a plastic relief, whereas the others are weakly engraved. The mirror-image symmetry and the frontal representation of the central figures are typical traits. Scholars have quite rightly insisted on the stylistic relationship with the mosaics in Romanesque basilicas of the same period.

Literature: Lauer, "Le Trésor du Sancta Sanctorum," *Monuments Piot* 15 (1906–7): 66–71. Cempanari and Amodei, *La Scala Santa* (1963), p. 97. Ragghianti, *L'arte in Italia,* 2 (1968): col 493.

*72 Detail of the lid of the reliquary casket (plate 71): Christ Appears to the Disciples Behind Closed Doors.*

The biblical reference for the scene is John 20: 19–29. In the foreground of the representation, a wall of large rectangular blocks with a double door in the center. The risen Christ delineated after the Hellenistic model: beardless, in *tunica, clavi,* and *pallium,* holding the scroll of the Law in his left hand; the right hand raised in a gesture that may be benedictory or oratorial. In addition to the Virgin, thirteen male figures are shown, evidently the eleven disciples (excluding Judas) and "them that were with them" at Emmaus (Luke 24: 33).

*73 Detail of the reliquary casket (plate 71): Noli me tangere.*

The scene is identified by the two women at the sepulcher to whom Christ appeared on the day of his Resurrection (Luke 24:1). Following the iconography generally adopted after the seventh century, the sepulcher is represented as a domed structure. As in the other scenes, the Lord is beardless and holds a scroll in his left hand. One of the women has cast herself at his feet; the other (probably Mary Magdalen), whose headdress is adorned with a cross, stretches her arms out to him in a gesture of supplication. The scene was presumably executed by an assistant of the master who did most of the work on the lid. The figures are stiff, the perspective awkward (notice the tree, which seemingly grows out of the prostrate woman's head).

*74 Detail of the reliquary casket (plate 71): The Supper at Emmaus.*

Christ, seated in the middle, lays the consecrated bread in the veiled hands of the disciple who sits in a reverential attitude on the left. The other disciple's hands are also veiled. This Oriental custom, which was widely imitated in the West all through the Middle Ages, denotes the recipient or bearer of precious objects. The disciples sit on *sellae castrenses*. The perspective of the table is rather odd: it is viewed from above. On it is a cross-grooved loaf of a type also found in non-Christian art. Eleven places are marked around the edge of the table with three-pronged arrows. The tablecloth hangs down in front, its folds indicated by crosses.

*75 and 76 Inv. no. 1881. Reliquary cross with scenes from the childhood of Christ.* Gold and cloisonné enamel. 10 $^5/_8$ × 7 $^1/_8$ × 1 $^3/_8$″. Executed under Pope Paschal I (817–24). From the Sancta Sanctorum.

The illustration shows the back of the cross, which is divided by beaded strips of gold into five compartments. The clear, vivid colors of the enameled areas are separated by gold ridges that fix the design. The glassy paste varies in depth, giving the enamel translucent effects which the artist may not have intended. The style is vigorous. The brightness of the colors is heightened by their contrasts. There is an obvious tendency toward abstract rendering of the human figures.

The pictures represent scenes from Christ's childhood. Central compartment: the Nativity, with the Virgin recumbent, the Infant Jesus in swaddling clothes lying in the crib, the ox and the ass; above, the hand of God the Father (?); lower down, the newborn babe being bathed, with Saint Joseph at the far right, his head in his hand. Top section: the Annunciation and the Visitation. Left-hand section: the Flight into Egypt. Right-hand section: the Adoration of the Magi. Bottom section: the Presentation in the Temple and the Baptism. On the front of the cross, which may have been decorated with scenes from Christ's later life, are five small niches that were probably designed to hold relics of the True Cross. The inconography displays typical characteristics of early Christian art that were generalized after the fifth century. Around the sides runs an inscription with the name of Paschal I. Originally the reliquary rested on a cushion that was covered with the material reproduced in plate 91.

This cross is considered the most precious object in the Treasure of the Sancta Sanctorum. It is attributed to a Greek artist who worked in Rome (Volbach, Amodei).

Literature: Lauer, "Le Trésor du Sancta Sanctorum," *Monuments Piot* 15 (1906–7): 40–49. F. Stohlman, *Gli smalti del Museo Sacro Vaticano* (Vatican City, 1939), pp. 47–48. Volbach, *Il tesoro della Cappella Sancta Sanctorum*, Museo Sacro, Guida 4 (1941), p. 16. Cempanari and Amodei, *La Scala Santa* (1963), pp. 93–94. Ragghianti, *L'arte in Italia*, 2 (1968): col. 493.

*77 Side view of gold and enamel cross (plate 75), showing the inscription of Pope Paschal I.*

On the lateral panels, Paschal I's inscription read by Stohlman as: ACCIPE, QUAESO, A DOMINA MEA REGINA MUNDI, HOC VEXILLUM CRUCIS QUOD TIBI PASCHALIS EPISCOPUS OPTULIT. This and the reliquary reproduced in plate 71 prove how lively was devotion to the Virgin Mary in the days of Paschal I.

Literature: Stohlman, *Gli smalti del Museo Sacro Vaticano* (1939), p. 19. Volbach, *Il tesoro della Cappella Sancta Sanctorum*, Museo Sacro, Guida 4 (1941), p. 16.

*78–81 The gold and enamel cross (plate 75) in its silver box.* Casket in embossed and gilded silver (like that reproduced in plate 71). $11^3/_4 \times 7^7/_8 \times 2^3/_8$". Early 9th century. Executed in a Roman workshop. From the Sancta Sanctorum.

On the sides of the box: the lamb of God with the emblems of the Evangelists and scenes from Christ's childhood. These latter follow each other like a continuous story. Plate 79: the Annunciation, the Visitation, and the Nativity. Plate 80: a shepherd from Bethlehem with his flock (the Annunciation to the Shepherds) and the three Magi guided by the star to Jerusalem (the building on the right may represent Herod's palace). Plate 81: the Adoration of the Magi and the Presentation in the Temple. On the sliding lid Christ is represented enthroned, with a book in his left hand and his right hand raised in benediction, between Saint Peter and Saint Paul. The throne stands on a mountain from which flow the four rivers that irrigate the garden of Eden, represented by the flowers engraved in the foreground. At the top, in two roundels, the archangels Michael and Gabriel. The whole panel is framed by a beaded border. The two rings for sliding the lid are still extant. For stylistic considerations, see the commentary to plates 71–74.

Literature: Lauer, "Le Trésor du Sancta Sanctorum," *Monuments Piot* 15 (1906–7): 60–66. W. F. Volbach, *Itinerario*, Biblioteca Apostolica Vaticana, Museo Sacro, Guida 3 (Vatican City, 1936), p. 16. Cecchelli, *Vita di Roma nel Medio Evo* (1951–60), 1: 25. Ragghianti, *L'arte in Italia*, 2 (1968): col. 497.

*82–88 Inv. no. 586. Reliquary for the head of Saint Praxedes.* Silver. Sides embossed, lid engraved and enameled. $9^1/_2 \times 7^1/_2 \times 7^1/_2$". 11th century. From the Sancta Sanctorum.

Casket-shaped container. On the sides (plates 86, 88), full-length figures of saints represented in high relief, gilded: two on each side with their names engraved by their heads. On the lid, a gold rectangle (plate 83) with a scene in cloisonné enamel, very finely executed, of Christ enthroned between the Virgin and John the Baptist. All around, medallions with busts of saints (plates 84, 85), also enamel on gold, of which only three are still extant.

Stylistic traits date the reliquary from the eleventh century and point to Byzantine artists. The decoration gives no indication as to the original purpose of the casket—an argument against its having been expressly commissioned and for its having been imported.

The finest heads in the medallions are those of Saint Simon and Saint Thomas (plates 84, 85). The rich clothing, the telling gestures, and particularly the splendid colors give these pieces a very high artistic value. Among the figures embossed on the sides of the box, that of the theologian Saint Gregory of Nazianzus (plate 88) merits special mention for the supple composition, the free treatment of the rich drapery, and the vigorous workmanship.

The reliquary was opened at an early date and closed again by Pope Nicholas III (1277–80), who appended his seal with the symbolic figure of the fisherman (plate 87).

Literature: Lauer, "Le Trésor du Sancta Sanctorum," *Monuments Piot* 15 (1906–7): 73. Stohlman, *Gli smalti del Museo Sacro Vaticano* (1939), p. 48. W. F. Volbach, *L'arte bizantina nel Medioevo*, Biblioteca Apostolica Vaticana, Museo Sacro, Guida I (Rome, 1935), p. 13. Volbach, *Il tesoro della Capella Sancta Sanctorum*, Museo Sacro, Guida 4 (1941), pp. 16–17. Cecchelli, *Vita di Roma nel Medio Evo* (1951–60), 1: 29. W. F. Volbach, *La stauroteca di Monopoli* (Rome, 1969).

*89 Inv. no. 1898 a–b. Reliquary (right) with sliding lid (left).* Painted wood. $10^5/_8 \times 4^7/_8 \times 1^1/_4$". Second half of the 10th century. Byzantine. From the Sancta Sanctorum.

The inside of the box (on the right) has a deep recess in the shape of a double cross. The pictures represent Christ, the Virgin, two archangels, Saint Peter, and Saint Paul. The sliding lid is painted on both sides. The outside, here reproduced, depicts the figure of Saint John Chrysostom holding an open book in his hands with the text from John 15: 12 urging men to love one another. A Crucifixion is painted on the inner face of the lid, which was in contact with the relics.

The reliquary is unanimously considered a masterwork of the School of Constantinople at the peak of the so-called Byzantine Renaissance. It was painted in tempera by a master miniaturist. The high artistic value of the work is demonstrated by the monumental treatment of the saint's figure, the technical mastery, and the handling of the drapery, which is rendered without any of the chilly rigidity found in works of the eleventh century and later.

Literature: Lauer, "Le Trésor du Sancta Sanctorum," *Monuments*

*Piot* 15 (1906–7): 95–97. Volbach, *L'arte bizantina nel Medioevo,* Museo Sacro, Guida 1 (1935), pp. 11–12. Cecchelli, *Vita di Roma nel Medio Evo* (1951–60), 9–10: 646–648.

*90 Inv. no. 1244. Woven fabric with cock in medallion (detail).* Silk. Medallion 10¼ × 9⅛″. 6th–7th century. Sassanid. From the Sancta Sanctorum.

Woven silk material with two silk warp threads and six or seven wefts (Volbach). Ten colors. Motif repeated *(continuum ad infinitum).* Medallion with triple border: plaited band, heart-leaf pattern, and plain band. The excellent quality of the material is emphasized by the choice of colors and their contrasted combination. Because of its quality and rarity, the cloth was utilized for wrapping relics, without any reference to the motif of the cock. Datable from the end of the Sassanid period, although some scholars have recently given preference to the sixth century (Devoti).

Literature: Grisar, *Die römische Kapelle Sancta Sanctorum und ihr Schatz* (1908), p. 128. W. F. Volbach, *I tessuti del Museo Sacro Vaticano* (Vatican City, 1942), p. 45. Volbach, *Il tesoro della Cappella Sancta Sanctorum,* Museo Sacro, Guida 4 (1941), pp. 11–12. Cecchelli, *Vita di Roma nel Medio Evo* (1951–60), 5–6: 312. D. D. (Donata Devoti), in Ragghianti, *L'arte in Italia,* 2 (1968): col. 284.

*91 Inv. no. 1275. Woven fabric with winged horses (detail).* Silk. 12¼ × 8⅜″. 8th century. Byzantine. From the Sancta Sanctorum.

Woven silk fabric with winged horses on red ground, presumably arranged in superposed rows as continuous ornamental motif. Heads and hooves decked with long multicolored ribbons. Though their wings are spread, the horses seem to be walking at a slow pace. Not all the horses are the same size.

The cloth served to cover a wadding-filled cushion on which Paschal I's enameled reliquary cross (plate 75) rested. It was found in the silver container reproduced in plate 78. Traces of the devotional oil that was poured over the relic can still be seen. The motif of the winged horse was certainly of Sassanid origin. It had a religious significance in that area of which those who used the fabric later for Paschal I's reliquary cannot have been aware. Certain characteristics—the strong colors (stronger than otherwise usual in Persia) and the lack of knowledge of anatomical details—point to an eighth-century Byzantine copy of a Sassanid design.

Literature: Grisar, *Die römische Kapelle Sancta Sanctorum und ihr Schatz* (1908), p. 132. Volbach, *I tessuti del Museo Sacro Vaticano* (1942), p. 44. Volbach, *Il tesoro della Cappella Sancta Sanctorum,* Museo Sacro, Guida 4 (1941), p. 12; Guida 6, p. 14. Cecchelli, *Vita di Roma nel Medio Evo* (1951–60), 5–6: 289.

*92 Inv. no. 1275. Woven fabric with lion motif in medallion (detail).* Silk. 8th–9th century. Medallion 5 × 3½″. Byzantine. From the Sancta Sanctorum.

The motif of facing lions in medallions of irregular shape is repeated on a large cloth made of two pieces of material cut out of a larger context and neatly hemmed. The colors are distributed in horizontal stripes of orange and deep yellow, obviously due to the weaving technique.

Cecchelli dates the fabric to the seventh or eighth century and attributes it to a Chinese workshop. Devoti dates it to the ninth or tenth century. The stiff, awkward design, the taste for animal representation, the mathematical symmetry of the figures—all suggest an Asiatic model. Volbach proposes Persia during the Muslim period; von Falke, eastern Persia. A Sassanid origin would seem to be confirmed by the small number (only six) and the sobriety of the colors. The original use is not known, but the fact that this cloth comes from the Sancta Sanctorum denotes that it had a ritual function.

Literature: Grisar, *Die römische Kapelle Sancta Sanctorum und ihr Schatz* (1908), pp. 129–130. O. von Falke, *Kunstgeschichte der Seidenweberei* (Berlin, 1936), pp. 20–21. Volbach, *I tessuti del Museo Sacro Vaticano* (1942), p. 43. Volbach, *Stoffe Medioevali,* Museo Sacro, Guida 6 (1943), p. 13. Cecchelli, *Vita di Roma nel Medio Evo* (1951–60), 5–6: 311–314. D. D. (Donata Devoti), in Ragghianti, *L'arte in Italia,* 2 (1968): cols. 283–285.

*93 Inv. no. 1258. Woven fabric with the Nativity in medallion (fragment).* Silk. 12⅜ × 10⅛″; diameter of medallion 11¾″. 7th–8th century. From the Sancta Sanctorum.

*94 Inv. no. 1231. Woven fabric with the Annunciation in medallion (detail).* Silk. 13¼ × 27″; diameter of medallion 12¾″. 7th–8th century. From the Sancta Sanctorum.

Plates 93 and 94 illustrate part of a piece of silk on which the same motifs are repeated. The figured scenes are set in a pattern of linked circles. The roundels are framed by a floral motif on a pale ground with beaded edge (small pale circles alternating with colored ellipses). The scenes stand out against a red ground. The linear style does not exclude a certain sculptural quality.

Iconographically, both scenes reveal the influence of Eastern Christendom, while the ornamental motifs point to Alexandria. The material may be part of the *veste* that Pope Leo III (795–816) donated to the altar of Saint Peter's, about which the *Liber Pontificalis* says: *In medio crucem de chrisoclabo cum orbicolis et rotas siricas habentes storias Adnuntiatione seu Natale domini nostri Jesu Christi.*

Literature: Grisar, *Die römische Kapelle Sancta Sanctorum und ihr Schatz* (1908), pp. 130–131. Volbach, *I tessuti del Museo Sacro Vaticano* (1942), pp. 39–40. Volbach, *Itinerario,* Museo Sacro, Guida 3 (1936), p. 12. W. F. Volbach and M. Hirmer, *Arte paleocristiana* (Florence, 1958), p. 115, no. 257. Cecchelli, *Vita di Roma nel Medio Evo* (1951–60), 5–6: 308. D. D. (Donata Devoti), in Ragghianti, *L'arte in Italia,* 2 (1968): cols. 283–284.

*95 Inv. no. 1250. Woven fabric with hunting scenes in medallion (detail).* Silk. 16⅝ × 13⅝″; diameter of medallion 12½″. 7th–8th century. From the Sancta Sanctorum.

Identical hunting scenes appear in large medallions linked by small floral discs. The design is clumsy and the motifs are arranged in exact mirror symmetry. Above: lion hunt around a tall, spreading palm tree. Below: leopard hunt. The red-stained areas on the beasts' front parts probably simulate wounds. Swift hounds take part in the chase. All empty spaces are filled with bird and plant motifs. The hunters wear a headdress topped with a cross. The fabric served to line a reliquary in which Jesus' sandals were kept.

The iconography points to the fifth century, but the awkward treatment of the figures, the insistent stylization of the subject, and certain details—the crosses, the *clavi* on the hunters' tunics, and the decorative motifs of the medallion borders—encourage the assumption that the material is a copy, perhaps executed in Constantinople, of a Sassanid model.

Literature: Grisar, *Die römische Kapelle Sancta Sanctorum und ihr Schatz* (1908), pp. 127–128. Volbach, *I tessuti del Museo Sacro Vaticano* (1942), pp. 44–45. Volbach, *Il tesoro della Cappella Sancta Sanctorum,* Museo Sacro, Guida 4 (1941), p. 12. Cecchelli, *Vita di Roma nel Medio Evo* (1951–60), 5–6: 313–314.

*96 Inv. no. 1315. Woven fabric with two lions and palm trees (detail).* Silk. $11^1/_8 \times 8^1/_8$″. 9th–10th century. From the Sancta Sanctorum.

The mirror symmetry of the pattern is exact down to the smallest details—the beasts' waving tails, their tongues, the stylized palm trees. This points to a classical model. The ornamental motifs of the circular border are the product of a slavish imitation, vague and inaccurate. Hence the attribution to the tenth century seems justified. The colors—reddish-brown ground and yellow pattern—are dull and lack contrast. Since the cloth was found in the Sancta Sanctorum, it presumably was connected with a reliquary.

Literature: Grisar, *Die römische Kapelle Sancta Sanctorum und ihr Schatz* (1908), p. 133. Volbach, *I tessuti del Museo Sacro Vaticano* (1942), p. 46. Volbach, *Stoffe Medioevali,* Museo Sacro, Guida 6 (1943), p. 14. Cecchelli, *Vita di Roma nel Medio Evo* (1951–60), 5–6: 316.

*97 Inv. no. 1247. Woven fabric with a man wrestling with a lion (fragment).* Silk. $7^3/_4 \times 6^1/_2$″. 7th–8th century. From the Sancta Sanctorum.

The male figure in a short tunic presses his right knee against the lion's back and pulls the beast's head toward him with both hands. The scene is framed by two arcs, above and below, which leave it open at the sides. This stylistic device gives the duel between man and beast a dynamic quality.

The fragment is part of a bag reliquary that was found full of bones. Figures and border are woven in the same four colors. The ornamental motifs of the border closely resemble those of the Annunciation in plate 94, but their execution is not nearly so good. This piece of cloth may be a product of the Christian East dating from the seventh or eighth century and based on a Syrian model. Cecchelli thinks it is sixth-century Alexandrian and represents one of the labors of Hercules. But it seems more apt to interpret the scene as an episode in the life of Samson or Daniel.

There is a specimen on the same theme at Dumbarton Oaks in which the group formed by lion and tamer is repeated in mirrored reflection, stressing the purely decorative nature of the pattern.

Literature: Grisar, *Die römische Kapelle Sancta Sanctorum und ihr Schatz* (1908), p. 133. Volbach, *I tessuti del Museo Sacro Vaticano* (1942), pp. 38–39. Volbach, *Stoffe Medioevali,* Museo Sacro, Guida 6 (1943), pp. 11–12. Cecchelli, *Vita di Roma nel Medio Evo* (1951–60), 5–6: 310.

*98–101 Inv. no. 590. Pyxis with scenes of Christ's miracles.* Ivory. Height $3^1/_8$″; diameter 5″. First half of the 6th century. From the Treasure of Milan Cathedral.

Originally the pyxis had a solid lock, traces of which can be seen in plate 99. Both the lid and the bottom are missing. Some of Christ's miracles are represented on the cylindrical surface. Plate 98: The Raising of Lazarus. Jesus strikes the tomb with a cross (instead of the customary *virga virtutis);* Lazarus' relatives are portrayed in attitudes of acclamation: the female figure behind Christ grasps the end of his *pallium.* Plate 99: two figures, perhaps Isaiah and David, an assumption borne out by comparison with a similar scene in the *Rossano Codex* and elsewhere. Plate 100: Jesus healing the blind boy before the door of a house or the gate of a city (Bethsaida)—or maybe a current architectural motif, for it is repeated in other scenes. Jesus is beardless and holds a cross in his left hand. The blind boy raises his left hand and leans on a stick grasped with his right hand. Plate 101: the healed paralytic of Capharnaum carrying his bed on his back.

The narrative is enlivened by the dynamic movement: not a single figure stands still. The bold relief against a neutral ground and the naturalistic, expressive attitudes are typical traits of popular Hellenistic art. That trend preserved the beardless, clothed type of Christ until the Middle Ages, as is proved by this pyxis. The work may be attributed to an Egyptian workshop, perhaps in Alexandria.

Literature: A. F. Gori, *Thesaurus veterum diptycorum,* 3 vols. (Florence, 1759), 3: 75–78. C. R. Morey, *Gli oggetti di avorio e di osso del Museo Sacro Vaticano* (Vatican City, 1936), pp. 59–60. W. F. Volbach, *Avori Medioevali,* Biblioteca Apostolica Vaticana, Museo Sacro, Guida 5 (Vatican City, 1942), pp. 4 and 6.

*102 Diptych with birds in grapevines.* Ivory. $7^1/_2 \times 3^1/_8 \times {}^1/_8$″. 10th century. Provenance unknown; probably from a Benedictine abbey.

Both panels are decorated with identical grapevines, which can be recognized as such although the leaves and fruit are stylized in the extreme. At the top, a bird pecks at a grape; in the middle, a large bunch of the fruit; at the bottom, another bird. The frame is a Greek fret interrupted by leaf motifs. This type of "assonometric" fret was current in painting about A.D. 1000. The character *(horror vacui)* and style of the work link it with those produced in the Abbey of Saint Gall, Switzerland.

Literature: Volbach, *Avori Medioevali,* Museo Sacro, Guida 5 (1942), p. 8.

*103–104 Inv. no. 628 a–b. The Rambona Diptych.* Ivory. $12^1/_4 \times 5^3/_8 \times {}^1/_4$″. c. 900 (Morey). Mentioned in the inventory of Pope Clement XIII (1758–69). From the Museo Buonarroti.

Left-hand panel, top: in a medallion borne by angels, Christ (bearded but without halo) makes the sign of blessing with his right hand and holds a book in his left. This may refer to the Ascension (or to a *Majestas)*, as seems indicated by the scene carved beneath it. Center: the Crucifixion, with Christ represented as *Christus Triumphans*. The Virgin points to her crucified Son with her right hand and, like John, holds her other hand to her cheek in a gesture of grief. Above the arms of the cross, the sun and the moon personified, also in an attitude of grief. At the bottom: supporting the stylized Calvary, the Roman she-wolf with Romulus and Remus, designated by the inscription.

Right-hand panel (divided into three parts), top: Virgin and Child enthroned, flanked by seraphim (plate 104). Center: three holy confessors, identified by the inscription as Gregory, Silvester, and Flavianus, framed by twining vines and foliage. The inscription announces that Abbot Odelricus commissioned the diptych for the convent by Ageltruda at Rambona. Bottom: probably the donor (Volbach and Ragghianti) with torch and palm frond.

Both panels end at the bottom with an ornament that recalls a crenelated crown *(merlatura)* and is certainly of Islamic origin. Volbach suggests that the ivory was imported from the Muslim East and subsequently worked over and adorned with Christian scenes. Traces of the original coloring can still be seen.

This unique work proves that the tradition of Rome was still alive even at so late a period when many alien trends were encroaching. It may have been executed by an artist from central Italy subjected to Lombardic influences. Evidence of this is the shallowness of the relief, the facial types, and the decorative interlacings used to fill every empty space. But the frontality and iteration of the figures indicate that the sculptor had also assimilated Byzantine models, while maintaining a certain freedom reflected in the varying treatment of the robes of the three holy bishops.

Literature: F. Buonarroti, *Osservazioni sopra alcuni frammenti di vasi antichi di vetro ornati di figure, trovati nei Cimiteri di Roma* (Florence, 1716), p. 257. F. Hermanin, "Il dittico di Rambona," in *Archivio della R. Societa Romana di Storia Patria* 21 (1898): 221–237. Morey, *Gli oggetti di avorio e di osso del Museo Sacro Vaticano* (1936), pp. 60–62. G. Fammilume, *La Badia di Rambona* (Tolentino, 1938), pp. 19–24. Volbach, *Avori Medioevali*, Museo Sacro, Guida 5 (1942), p. 11. Cecchelli, *Vita di Roma nel Medio Evo* (1951–60), 4: 232–236. Ragghianti, *L'arte in Italia*, 2 (1968), col. 493.

*105 Inv. no. 2233. Book cover: The Nativity*. Ivory. $6^3/_8 \times 5^1/_4 \times {}^1/_4$". 10th–11th century. Provenance unknown.

The little panel tells the story of Christ's birth. Top left: the arrival of the Magi guided by the star, which points to the swaddled Infant warmed by the ox and the ass. The crib is adorned with a heavy beaded molding. The scene of the Infant being bathed, to which the musing Joseph turns his back, is overshadowed by the recumbent Virgin. Along the left-hand edge, an angel gives the glad tidings to a shepherd.

The typically Eastern iconography is preserved in Slavonic works of a far later date. The technique of the carving is quite remarkable. The artist was careful to hollow out the ivory behind the figures, so that they are executed almost in the round and seem here and there (for example, the Infant's head, the Virgin's couch) to be entirely detached from the background. But the relief is undercut: every point is lower than the level of the frame. This produces a vividly pictorial effect. The artist displays a strong naturalistic bent, as is evidenced by both the animal and the human figures. The empty space above the Virgin's head is filled with a highly stylized shrub. The work is undoubtedly the product of a Byzantine workshop.

Literature: R. Kanzler, *Gli avori dei Musei Profano e Sacro della Biblioteca Vaticana* (Rome, 1903), II, no. 26. Morey, *Gli oggetti di avorio e di osso del Museo Sacro Vaticano* (1936), p. 64. Volbach, *L'arte bizantina nel Medioevo,* Museo Sacro, Guida 1 (1935), p. 16.

*106–110 Inv. no. 49 (De' Rossi). Paneled cover of a gospel book.* Ivory. $14^7/_8 \times 10^7/_8 \times {}^1/_8$". 9th century (Volbach); 10th century (Morey). From the Abbey of Saint Nazarius at Lorsch, Germany.

The five panels of the ivory relief are fastened together by a frame in gilded copper (plate 106), which was added at a later date. The top and bottom panels are carved in the same ivory, which differs from that of the three panels in the middle. The lower edge of the top panel (plate 108) is trimmed at right and left to fit those that lie directly beneath it. It shows two angels holding a medallion with a Greek cross. On the central panel of the middle row, a beardless Christ flanked by a serpent and a basilisk tramples underfoot a lion and a dragon. His right hand is raised in an oratorial or benedictory gesture; his left hand holds a book. On each side panel, an angel with scepter and scroll. The bottom panel (plates 107 and 109) tells the story of the three wise men from the East: we see them being dispatched by King Herod and offering their gifts to the Infant Jesus.

This splendid carving is unanimously viewed as a Carolingian work and attributed to the Palace School. It reflects the aims of the so-called Carolingian Renaissance. (Charlemagne cherished the antique repertory of art and literature and preserved it from destruction.) The angels on the top panel (plate 108) are obviously inspired by antique "Victories"; the rosettes at the sides derive from a fifth-century (egg-and-dart) motif. On the other hand, early Christian motifs can be recognized in the scene carved on the bottom panel. Typical is the questioning gesture (the forefinger on the lower lip) of the second Magus (plate 109): it frequently occurs in representations of Saint Peter denying Christ. The whole work is embellished by the rich architectural setting.

The Saviour and the angels (plates 106 and 110) denote a classicistic vision and a culture that developed in monasteries under the aegis of Charlemagne. The decorative elements, particularly the pseudo-Corinthian capitals, which derive from late antique models, reveal a lack of knowledge and comprehension of classical art.

Originally this ivory was the front cover of a Gospel Book, the back of which is now in the Victoria and Albert Museum, London. Morey suggests that the top section was part of a fifth-century consular diptych. It is obviously superior to the rest of the work. He holds that the remaining sections were worked over at the directions of Abbot Salamann of Lorsch (972–98) in the workshop of the Reichenau monastery. Volbach, instead, considers the whole carving as a ninth-century product executed by a single artist.

Literature: Kanzler, *Gli avori dei Musei Profano e Sacro della Biblioteca Vaticana* (1903), II, no. 21. Morey, *Gli oggetti di avorio e di osso del Museo Sacro Vaticano* (1936), pp. 11–16 and 62–64. Volbach, *Avori Medioevali*, Museo Sacro, Guida 5 (1942), pp. 7–8.

*111–112 Inv. no. 721. Book cover: Christ in Glory Between Angels and Saints.* Ivory. $9^3/_8 \times 5 \times {}^3/_8$". 12th century. From the Camaldolite Monastery of Avellana (via the convent of San Michele on Murano). Worked up as part of a book cover. One of the missing panels is in Ravenna, the other in a French private collection.

Christ enthroned in a mandorla borne by three winged angels. On his thigh rests a book with the inscription: EGO SUM RESURRECCIO ET VITA (I am resurrection and life). His right hand is raised in the Greek gesture of benediction. On the three visible branches of the cross in the nimbus, the letters REX (King). The two angels at the top are a cherub and a seraph; the third, at the bottom, is not identified. In the bottom corners Saints Gervase and Protase.

The refined execution and the quality of the carving are remarkable. Nonetheless, one must not overlook certain weak points, such as the Saviour's left hand, which has a rather vague grip on the book. The ivory is apparently a Lombard work; this assumption is supported by the two saints, who were particularly revered in Milan.

Literature: Gori, *Thesaurus veterum diptycorum* (1759), 3: 69. Morey, *Gli oggetti di avorio e di osso del Museo Sacro Vaticano* (1936), pp. 68–70. Volbach, *Avori Medioevali*, Museo Sacro, Guida 5 (1942), p. 11.

*113–118 Inv. no. 610. Byzantine triptych.* Ivory. $10^1/_2 \times 13^1/_4$ (open; $6^1/_2$ closed) $\times {}^1/_2$". 11th–12th century (Morey); 10th century (Volbach). From a private collection at Todi acquired by Pope Benedict XIV (1740–58). Mentioned in the inventory of Pope Clement XIII (1758–69).

The inner faces of the three panels (plate 115) are carved in accordance with a uniform plan; two rows of full-length figures are separated by a row of roundels *(tondi)*. The same arrangement recurs on the outer faces of the two lateral leaves (plate 114). In the rectangular upper compartment of the inner side, the *Majestas Domini* (plates 113, 115): Christ enthroned, flanked by Saint John and the Virgin on raised platforms, holds a book with his left hand and raises his right hand in an oratorial gesture; behind the throne, the archangels Michael and Gabriel. The figure of Christ and his extremely ornate throne are viewed from three-quarters. The saints in the lower compartment stand in a row with their heads at exactly the same level (isocephaly); the roundels, too, are almost identical. The figures on the two side panels are slightly farther apart. On the back of the center panel (plate 114) is a gemmed cross set in a festoonery pattern adorned with birds and floral motifs (plate 118). Traces of coloring and gilding—both original and later—are still clear to see, particularly on the armed men at the top of the inside lateral leaves (plate 115).

This was evidently a highly prized work, perhaps a small portable altar. The apparent uniformity of the various elements gives the composition a distinctive rhythm, which is stressed by differences of form and proportions (the full-length figures and the busts in the roundels) and also of spacing. The *Majestas* group has a rhythm all its own, which contrasts with that of the other figures. Similarly, on the back, the vividly pictorial quality of the cross is set off by the clear-cut figures of the two pairs of saints at either side.

The modeling, the drapery, and the execution (which is extremely free despite the exact typification of the figures, for example, that of Saint Clement of Ancyra, plate 117) denote the style and experience of an outstanding artist trained in a Constantinople workshop. The hieratic composure of the whole work emphasizes its closeness to "classical" Byzantine models and confirms its dating to the tenth century.

Literature: Gori, *Thesaurus veterum diptycorum* (1759), 3: 217–219. Morey, *Gli oggetti di avorio e di osso del Museo Sacro Vaticano* (1936), pp. 65–67. Volbach, *L'arte bizantina nel Medioevo*, Museo Sacro, Guida 1 (1935), pp. 15–16. Volbach, *La Croce: Lo sviluppo nell'oreficeria sacra*, Museo Sacro, Guida 2 (1938), p. 9.

*119 Inv. no. 639. Crucifixion.* Ivory. $7 \times 3^7/_8 \times {}^1/_2$". 12th century. From the Cistercian abbey of Rathausen, acquired in 1851.

The scene is represented in accordance with the usual iconography. The cross, which is the focal point of the composition (it is painted to imitate wood), bears Christ's dead body. His head is slightly bowed, his feet are splayed. At the sides, the Virgin and Saint John with hand on cheek to signify grief. Higher up, the emblems of the four Evangelists with the sun and the moon.

The lively colors are partly disintegrated. The forms are static but not rigid, ponderous but not devoid of naturalism. They justify the attribution of the work to a Tuscan artist of the Romanesque period who was out of touch with the major artistic centers. This Tuscan origin finds confirmation in the classicistic capital letters of the inscription at the top of the cross.

Literature: Kanzler, *Gli avori dei Musei Profano e Sacro della Biblioteca Vaticana* (1903), II, no. 20. Morey, *Gli oggetti di avorio e di osso del Museo Sacro Vaticano* (1936), pp. 73–74. Volbach, *Avori Medioevali*, Museo Sacro, Guida 5 (1942), pp. 11–12.

*120 Inv. no. 1191. Saint Theodore of Tyre.* Mosaic. $5^1/_2 \times 2^1/_2$". 11th–12th century (Volbach); 13th–14th century (Charulambous-Mouriki). Provenance unknown.

The little icon represents Saint Theodore of Tyre; in the inscription he is termed soldier, general, and martyr. Objects of this type designed for private devotion were often exchanged as gifts.

The execution of the mosaic is extremely fine. The minute stone cubes, each measuring about half a millimeter across, are set in a layer of wax. The whole is surrounded by a wooden frame. The brilliant colors and the elaborate delineation of costume and attributes—the face is treated in a more sculptural manner—warrant the attribution of the work to the best period of what is often termed the second golden age of Byzantine art.

Literature: *Catalogo della Mostra dell'arte bizantina* (Grottaferrata, 1905), pp. 169–170. A. Muñoz, *L'art byzantin à l'exposition de Grottaferrata* (Rome, 1906), p. 176, fig. 136. Volbach, *L'arte bizantina nel Medioevo*, Museo Sacro, Guida 1 (1935), p. 12. Cecchelli, *Vita di Roma nel Medio Evo* (1951–60), 2: 73. D. Charulambous-Mouriki, in *Byzantine Art*, catalogue of the exhibition of Byzantine art in Athens (Athens, 1964), p. 235, no. 165.

*121 Inv. no. 982. Saint Theodore Stratelates in prayer.* Steatite. $8^1/_2 \times 4^5/_8$″. 13th century (11th–12th, Righetti; 12th, Volbach). Provenance unknown; perhaps Venice (Cecchelli).

The saint is viewed from three-quarters; he stands erect with his hands raised in prayer. The pointed beard is a feature of the iconography of this saint, whereas the hair style with its tight little curls is typical of icons of the early eleventh century. Over his coat of mail, Theodore wears a cloak *(chlamys?)* that discloses the hilt of the sword hanging at his right side—an interesting detail, because the sword was usually worn on the left side.

The lance and shield are treated as attributes, for they are quite unrelated to the saint's figure. The shield is actually a heraldic escutcheon of a type current in the West during the late Middle Ages, and is probably an allusion to the owner of the icon. This confirms the assumption that the work was executed in Venice, where the relics of Saint Theodore were brought in 1260, by an artist who was a native of Constantinople or had been trained there. The shallow relief is typical of sculpture in steatite, a tough compact stone. The artist has mastered his material and made the most of its potentialities. Originally, the figure stood under an arch supported by two slender columns. The one on the right is still extant; the other has been replaced by a late copy in wood.

Literature: Muñoz, *L'art byzantin à l'exposition de Grottaferrata* (1906), pp. 118–119. Volbach, *L'arte bizantina nel Medioevo*, Museo Sacro, Guida 1 (1935), p. 17. Righetti, *Opere di Glittica dei Musei Sacro e Profano*, Museo Sacro, Guida 7 (1955), p. 31. Charulambous-Mouriki, in *Byzantine Art*, catalogue of the exhibition in Athens (1964), pp. 201–202.

*122 Inv. no. 723. Saint Pantaleimon.* Steatite. $5^1/_2 \times 4^1/_2$″. 12th century (10th–11th, Righetti). From a Basilian monastery in the south of Italy (Muñoz).

Though Bertelli sees this figure as Saint Luke, it can be identified as Pantaleimon (Pantaleon; d. 305), patron saint of physicians, through the resemblance to unquestionable portraits on Oriental icons where the saint's small face is always framed by a quantity of tight curls. Here he is set under an arch supported by two slender spiral columns. This and other details, such as the hair style, stress the stylistic affinity of the work with the Saint Theodore of plate 121 and permit this icon to be dated to the late twelfth century. Saint Pantaleimon holds the attributes of a surgeon—an instrument case and a long curved instrument that tapers to a point. The youthful figure is richly dressed in sleeved tunic and *colobium*.

The relief is set in a painted wooden panel surrounded by ten far smaller tablets (the lower portions of two of these are visible at the top of plate 122). These latter represent Christ flanked by two archangels, the Virgin, and Saint John; lower down, an unidentified saint surrounded by four scenes from his life. Clumsily painted on the panel are the Annunciation, Mary Magdalen, and Mary the Egyptian (Righetti).

Literature: Muñoz, *L'art byzantin à l'exposition de Grottaferrata* (1906), pp. 120–123, fig. 85. Volbach, *L'arte bizantina nel Medioevo*, Museo Sacro, Guida 1 (1935), p. 17. Righetti, *Opere di Glittica dei Musei Sacro e Profano*, Museo Sacro, Guida 7 (1955), pp. 32–33.

*123–124 Inv. no. 1177. Relief in "pietra dura," obverse and reverse.* $2^3/_8 \times 1^3/_4$″. 13th century. Provenance unknown.

The devotional medallion is carved on both sides. On one side, the archangel Gabriel; on the other, the Virgin in an affectionate pose *(Glykophilousa)*, tenderly pressing her cheek against that of the Infant Jesus. Two different artists may have carved the piece; the Virgin is superior in quality.

The design of the lettering (the figures are identified by the usual signs and symbols; the inscription over the Virgin's head has not yet been deciphered), the unfinished ornamental motif in the Virgin's nimbus, and particularly the stylistic peculiarities make this beyond doubt a provincial Byzantine work executed not earlier than the second half of the thirteenth century.

Literature: Volbach, *L'arte Bizantina nel Medioevo*, Museo Sacro, Guida 1 (1935), p. 18. Righetti, *Opere di Glittica dei Musei Sacro e Profano*, Museo Sacro, Guida 7 (1955), pp. 27–28.

*125 Inv. no. 1162. Christ Enthroned.* Green jasper. $2^5/_8 \times 2$″. 12th century. Provenance unknown.

Christ as Pankrator is seated on a large, richly decorated, backless throne. In the top corners, two roundels with busts of the archangels Michael and Gabriel, identified by inscriptions. The depth of the relief diminishes toward the top until in the cross on the nimbus it is barely perceptible. It is very bold again in the roundels with the archangels. These variations in the depth of the relief cannot be attributed to the original piece of unworked jasper: they show that the artist aimed at achieving certain effects of perspective.

The work reveals a sense of plastic and spatial values. Observe, for instance, the large empty space between the roundels and the chair cushion. There is less feeling for draftsmanship, as witnessed by the lines, all of which are more or less vertical or horizontal; this gives the work a certain rigidity. Undoubtedly executed by a Byzantine artist, perhaps in Italy.

Literature: *L'arte Bizantina nel Medioevo*, Museo Sacro, Guida 1 (1935), p. 17. Righetti, *Opere di Glittica dei Musei Sacro e Profano*, Museo Sacro, Guida 7 (1955), pp. 25–26.

*126 Inv. no. 1160. Christ in a Mandorla.* Red jasper. $2^5/_8 \times 2^1/_4$″. 13th century (14th or 15th, Righetti). Provenance unknown.

Christ stands on a raised platform in a mandorla, on which are inscribed the letters IC–XC (Jesus Christus). His head is backed by a pearl-edged nimbus adorned with a cross. At each side, arranged to fit the curvature of the mandorla, angels with the instruments of the Passion (cross, sponge, lance, nails, crown of thorns); at the top, two archangels with the labarum. The iconographic composition recalls representations of the Last Judgment.

Although linearity is the chief trait of this work—all the figures are elongated and symmetrically arranged to fit the curve of the mandorla—a sense of plastic effect is revealed in the hollowed-out mandorla, where the illusion of depth is enhanced by the painterly contrast of light and shade. This sculptural sensibility derives from Byzantine models executed after the tenth century. It is reflected in the curious, geometrical effect produced by the adherence of the drapery to the bodies, for example, on the knees of the two angels in the foreground. The platform does not present the reversed perspective usual in Byzantine art. On the basis of these antitheses the work might be attributed to a Venetian artist who was very close to the Gothic style of the late thirteenth century.

Literature: Righetti, *Opere di Glittica dei Musei Sacro e Profano*, Museo Sacro, Guida 7 (1955), p. 40.

*127 Inv. no. 1101. Reliquary cross.* Gold. $1^{5}/_{8} \times 1^{1}/_{8} \times {}^{1}/_{4}''$. 5th–6th century. Rome.

A Latin cross with splayed arms executed in the finest niello technique and decorated with classical motifs. The ornamental tracery is interrupted, on both front and back, by strips of vertical and horizontal lettering. Obverse, horizontally: *EMMANOYHA* (Emmanuel), the name given Our Lord in Matthew 1 : 23; vertically: NOBISCUM DEUS (God with us), the interpretation of that name in the same Gospel. Reverse, horizontally: MORS INIMICE TIBI; vertically: CRUX EST VITA MI[HI] (Death for thee, oh enemy, the cross is life for me). The monograms at the ends of the arms have not yet been deciphered.

A small ring is screwed onto the top of the cross; when it is removed, the cross opens revealing a hollow in which a relic may be kept. This devotional object, which was obviously meant to be worn around the neck, was found in Rome in 1863 in a grave close to the church of San Lorenzo fuori le Mura. It lay on the breast of a man who had been dead for centuries.

This work is a most important document for the Christian cult during the first centuries of our era. In fact, it proves that the cross was attributed with exorcistic powers and viewed as a pledge of Salvation and a refuge from the enemy. In all probability this specimen was made by a Roman goldsmith who was an expert at niello work. The niello (a paste made with sulphur and lead) used to fill the interstices in the tracery is still intact. The precise execution of the ornamental motif, which is copied from classical models, proves the artist's skill. The rather rigid design warrants the attribution of the precious object to the fifth or early sixth century.

Literature: G. B. de' Rossi, "La Croce d'oro rinvenuto nella basilica di S. Lorenzo," *Bullettino di archeologia cristiana* (1863), pp. 33–38. Volbach, *La Croce: Lo sviluppo nell'oreficeria sacra*, Museo Sacro, Guida 2 (1938), pp. 6–7. Cecchelli, *Vita di Roma nel Medio Evo* (1951–60), 1 : 15–16; 11 : 742–743.

*128 Inv. no. 623 (De' Rossi). Votive cross.* Bronze. $18^{7}/_{8} \times 12^{7}/_{8} \times 2^{3}/_{8}''$. 5th–6th century. Provenance unknown.

A large openwork cross with Greek inscription: in memory of the dead Olympius. The letters incised at the junction of the arms signify: Jesus Christ, Son of God, Christ sole light. These inscriptions give the cross an exorcistic character. A minute cross is attached at each end of the crosspiece; under it a ring acts as counterweight.

Its unusual size leads to the presumption that this was a processional cross. Observe its proportions: the ratio of height to breadth is the same as in the gold cross in plate 127. The provenance is not known, but the inscription seems to denote that it came from a grave.

Literature: Volbach, *La Croce: Lo sviluppo nell'oreficeria sacra*, Museo Sacro, Guida 2 (1938), p. 6. Cecchelli, *Vita di Roma nel Medio Evo* (1951–60), 11 : 742–744.

*129 and 130 Inv. nos. 1097 and 1098. Votive crosses.* Gold. Plate 129: $3 \times 2^{3}/_{8}''$. Plate 130: $3^{1}/_{4} \times 2^{3}/_{4}''$. 6th–7th century. Provenance unknown.

Two typical specimens of the Longobard period, and at the same time remarkable examples of so-called barbarian art. The shape and pattern were obtained by hammering the gold sheet *(bractea)* on a wooden core. Designed for sewing on a garment: observe the small holes at the corners of the central square (plate 130) and at the ends of the arms. The tracery displays the pronounced linear character typical of the sculpture of that period.

Literature: H. Leclercq, "Croix et Crucifix," in *Dictionnaire d'Archéologie chrétienne et de Liturgie* (Paris, 1914), vol. 3, p. 2, cols. 3097–3102. P. Toesca, *Il Medioevo*, vol. 1 of *Storia dell'arte Italiana*, pp. 324–327. Volbach, *La Croce: Lo sviluppo nell'oreficeria sacra*, Museo Sacro, Guida 2 (1938), p. 7.

*131 Inv. no. 1837 a–b. Pectoral reliquary cross.* Gilded and enameled bronze. $4^{1}/_{8} \times 3^{1}/_{4}''$. 9th–10th century. Provenance unknown.

This work is an *encolpium:* a pectoral cross for containing relics. The two parts are joined together by a hinge at the foot. On the front are five busts enclosed in roundels: in the center, Christ between the Virgin and Saint John; at the top, Saint Sergius; at the bottom, Saint Paul. The roundels are executed in cloisonné enamel, the rest of the cross in champlevé enamel. The personages portrayed in the roundels are identified by the usual symbols. On the back, which is in bad condition, one can recognize Christ between the Virgin and Saint John in the central roundel, two angels in the others.

The tradition for objects of this sort was lost during the iconoclastic troubles. As a result, the colors of the enamel, though varied, lack the brilliance of earlier works and still more of later ones. The cross was executed by a Byzantine goldsmith.

Literature: Muñoz, *L'art byzantin à l'exposition de Grottaferrata* (1906), p. 162. Volbach, *L'arte Bizentina nel Medioevo*, Museo Sacro, Guida 1 (1935), p. 13. Stohlman, *Gli smalti del Museo Sacro Vaticano* (1939), p. 49.

*132–133 Inv. no. 1102. Pectoral reliquary cross, obverse and reverse.* Gilded bronze. $5 \times 3^{1}/_{8} \times {}^{5}/_{8}''$. 10th–11th century (6th–7th, Cecchelli).

On the obverse, Christ on the Cross wearing a sleeveless tunic *(colobium)*; at the ends of the crosspiece, the Virgin and Saint John; at the top, the sun and the moon. The usual cartouche above Christ's head has become a rectangle with intersecting diagonals on a dotted field; the symmetrical extensions on the four sides of the rectangle bear no relation to the rest of the cross. The text of John 19:26, "Behold thy son; behold thy mother," is inscribed in Greek beneath Christ's arms. His feet, which are placed side by side, rest on a sort of cushion. On the reverse, the Virgin and Child flanked by the inscription in Greek: "The Holy Mother of God." At the four ends of the cross, roundels with the four Evangelists.

The robe worn by the crucified Christ *(colobium)* was not customary either in the first centuries of the Christian era or in the late Middle Ages. This is important for dating the work, which could only have been executed between the fifth century and the eleventh. But the cushion under Christ's feet, his bowed head and closed eyes, the plastic handling of the Virgin's robe, and the flowing lines of the drapery point to the tenth or eleventh century. The cross was made by a Byzantine artist who may have worked in Rome.

Literature: Grimonard de Saint-Laurent, "Iconographie de la croix et du crucifix," *Annales Archéologiques* 26 (1869): 142. E.S. King, "The Date and Provenance of a Bronze Reliquary Cross in the Museo Cristiano," *Memorie della Pontificia Accademia Romana di Archeologia* 2 (1928): 193–194. Volbach, *La Croce: Lo sviluppo nell'oreficeria sacra*, Museo Sacro, Guida 2 (1938), p. 7. Cecchelli, *Vita di Roma nel Medio Evo* (1951–60), 2: 743.

*134 Inv. no. 1100. Pectoral cross.* Gold. 2³/₄ (without the ring) × 2¹/₄ × ¹/₄″. 6th–7th century. Found in the ruins of the church of Sant'Agapito at Palestrina.

The cross is embossed. The outline is curved so as to frame the roundels at the ends. The beardless Christ is represented in the posture of crucifixion, but the cross itself is lacking or merely hinted at behind his arms. The nail holes in his hands and feet are greatly exaggerated. Above his head the letters ICX, an unusual abbreviation of the name Jesus; the letters are preceded by a swastika.

The roundels at the ends of the crossbeam each contain a bust of a saint: bearded on the left, beardless on the right. Those at the ends of the vertical shaft have two busts each, those at the bottom differing greatly from the rest. The figures are turned toward each other as if in an embrace; their robes are draped in a manner at once sculptural and painterly. The robes of the other figures, including that of Christ, are all decorated in the same way: with serried rows of small horizontal lunettes interrupted by the vertical bands of the *clavi*.

The clumsy execution reveals a "barbarian" manner. But the iconographic details, for instance the beardless Christ, are obviously of Byzantine derivation (except for the two figures in the roundel at the foot). This work is adequate evidence of the use of images of Christ on the Cross in connection with burials—a custom whose exorcistic character is stressed by the presence of the swastika. It was found in the ruins of a church dedicated to Saint Agapitus at Palestrina.

Literature: C. Marucchi, in *Nuovo Bullettino d'Archeologia Cristiana* (1899), pp. 225–244. Volbach, *La Croce: Lo sviluppo nell'oreficeria sacra*, Museo Sacro, Guida 2 (1938), p. 7. Cecchelli, *Vita di Roma nel Medio Evo* (1951–60), 1: 16; 2: 743.

*135 Inv. no. 616 (De' Rossi). Pectoral cross.* Bronze. 3¹/₈ (with ring) × 2¹/₈″. Late 7th century (?). Provenance unknown.

In this peculiar object the cross seems as if molded on the figure of the crucified Christ. It reflects the tendency—in accordance with an ancient custom also found among the early Christians—of giving inanimate objects the shape of the human figure. Here the process has produced a quality that makes the object extremely difficult to date.

An almost identical specimen is in the Damascus Museum. Such crosses were probably made at the time of the Islamic conquest of the East, when Christian art was all but wiped out. Hence they may be viewed as the product of a late "primitivism." The cross reproduced here can hardly be earlier than the end of the seventh century, when the capital of the Omniad empire was established at Damascus. Some scholars view this cross as a northern work from pre-Romanesque times; they date it to the eighth or ninth century and attribute it to a locality where direct Longobard influence was not felt.

Literature: E. Coche de la Ferté, *L'antiquité chrétienne du Musée du Louvre* (Paris, 1958).

*136 Inv. no. 840 (De' Rossi). Enameled crucifix.* Gilded copper with champlevé enamel. 9¹/₂ × 7¹/₂″. 13th century. Mentioned in the inventory of Clement XIII (1758–69). Fromt the Museo Vettori.

Originally the figure of Christ was attached to a wooden cross. He is portrayed as still alive: the eyes are wide open, the pupils represented by two small red stones. In accordance with a style current in the thirteenth century, the muscles of the torso are indicated by schematically incised lines. The knees are slightly bent; the feet are firmly planted on a footrest. The crown topped by a small cross originally had four jutting florets. The loincloth hangs down very low, particularly at the back. The girdle is richly decorated with champlevé enamel; the hollows of the drapery are filled with an enamel similar to that of Limoges. The original gilding is preserved only in the parts that do not protrude.

The ornamentation shows a linear tendency. The body is slightly twisted, matching the inclination of the head; the legs are viewed exactly from the front. The whole work shows a naturalistic conception, but the girdle is decorated in traditional Byzantine fashion. These traits reveal a French origin not later than the thirteenth century.

Literature: L. Boudery, "Orfèvrerie et émaillerie limousines au Vatican," *Bulletin de la Société Archéologique et Historique du Limousin* 47 (1899): 352, 354, 368. Stohlman, *Gli smalti del Museo Sacro Vaticano* (1939), pp. 38–39.

*137 Inv. no. 1951. Crucifix.* Bronze. 9¹/₂ × 7⁷/₈″. Late 12th century. Provenance unknown.

Originally the body was attached to a wooden cross. The portrayal of the crucified Christ makes no attempt to imitate reality; the deformation of the outer appearance is aimed rather at expressing the inner substance of the image. The limbs are exaggeratedly long and thin, as if weightless; they contrast with the huge head, whose size is enhanced by the beard and crown. It is caught at the moment when it droops in the death throes, and this makes it seem heavier still. The elongated body is articulated by fine, incised lines which are thicker in the decoration of the crown and loincloth. This latter has a knot in front which derives from a typical early Romanesque form but has no apparent function here. The work is of excellent quality and may be attributed to the Rhenish school of the end of the twelfth century.

Literature: Volbach, *La Croce: Lo sviluppo nell'oreficeria sacra,* Museo Sacro, Guida 2 (1938), p. 9.

*138–140 Christ Enthroned with Apostles.* Copper, embossed, gilded, and partly adorned with enamel and gems. Plate 138 (Inv. nos. 857, 838, 887): Christ Enthroned with Saint Peter and an Apostle. Christ $16^1/_8 \times 7^3/_4$″; Saint Peter $8^5/_8 \times 3^1/_4$″; the apostle $8^7/_8 \times 3$″. Plate 139 (Inv. no. 839): Saint Paul (?). Whole figure $8^5/_8 \times 3^1/_4$″; height of head, from crown to tip of beard, $2^1/_2$″; maximum width of head 1″. Plate 140 (Inv. nos. 886, 1416): Two Apostles. The apostle on the left $8^7/_8 \times 3$″; the apostle on the right $8^7/_8 \times 2^5/_8$″. 13th century. From the Altar of the Confessio in Saint Peter's, Rome.

The statuette of Christ is much larger than those of the apostles, but its thickness, particularly at the foot, is very small in proportion. This fact confirms the assumption that the statuettes are the survivors of the group of Christ with the Twelve Apostles which adorned the front of the Altar of the Confessio that stood directly above Saint Peter's tomb in the old basilica. Before the statuettes were set up, Pope Innocent III (1198–1216) had the altar front protected with a grating which is still there today. This left very little room for the statuettes, so their thickness had to be restricted; this is most evident in the figure of Christ. At a later date an inscription was engraved on the grating, which still reads: *Cum discipulis suis bis sex Christus . . .* This provides formal confirmation of the probable provenance of the statuettes.

The statuettes were originally mounted on a wooden framework, as proved by the nail holes that are still clear to see. They derive from well-known models (Christ's gesture, for example, is not oratorial but benedictory, after the Latin mode). Consequently, what distinguishes them is the ornamentation. The close-knit, incised lines result in a painterly design that moderates the plastic values. These latter are particularly evident in the image of Christ, where convex and concave are smoothly blended.

Beads of colored stone make bright eyes, while other gems adorn the robes and the books that some of the figures hold. But the chief merit of the little statues lies in the enamel applied by the Limoges technique over their entire surface. The metal lines fix the design, which must have been greatly emphasized when the gilding was intact. The artist used his colors with the utmost freedom, paying little heed to realism. For instance, the eyes of Saints Peter and Paul are green like their tunics. Blue, green, and red blend harmoniously, unhindered by lines of separation and enhanced by the red ground color which here and there shimmers through.

Literature: X. Barbier de Montault, *La Bibliothèque Vaticane et ses annexes* (Rome, 1867), p. 80. Stohlman, *Gli smalti del Museo Sacro Vaticano* (1939), pp. 14 and 33–34. Volbach, *Itinerario*, Museo Sacro, Guida 3 (1936), p. 27.

*141 Inv. no. 505. The crook of a bishop's crozier.* Copper, engraved, gilded, and enameled (Limoges). Height (from the base of the knob to the top of the crook) $12^5/_8$″; width (diameter of the spiral) $5^1/_8$″. 13th century. Provenance unknown.

In the crook, the Annunciation. The archangel Gabriel is portrayed alighting from his flight, with one foot still off the ground. On the knob, which is embellished with enamel, four small metal figures, possibly of the Evangelists. The crook grows out of the knob rather like a climbing plant. It has a crest of little crockets. Inside the crook, the tendrils protrude to support the figures. At the bottom, a tendril links up with the shaft of the crook.

The enamel, of the typical Limoges type, is framed by a lattice of metal strips that predominates over all the other elements of the decoration. The modeling of the figures is delicate and sensitive, particularly that of the archangel with its broken lines. The long necks and smooth drapery emphasize the Gothic character of the work.

Literature: X. Barbier de Montault, "Les crosses du Musée Chrétien du Vatican," *Revue de l'Art chrétien* 17 (1874): 32–34. Stohlman, *Gli smalti del Museo Sacro Vaticano* (1939), p. 37.

*142 Inv. no. 504. The crook of a bishop's crozier.* Copper, engraved, gilded, and enameled (Limoges). Height (from the base of the knob to the top of the crook) $7^1/_4$″; width $5^1/_4$″. 13th century. Provenance unknown. Mentioned in the inventory of Pope Clement XIII (1758–69).

Very like the crook of plate 141, but less elegant; perhaps slightly earlier. The metal lattice on the crook forms a homogeneous, delicate pattern. The outstanding feature is the turquoise blue of the enamel. In the center, the archangel Michael in the act of plunging his sword into the dragon, which grows out of the plant form of the crook. The shaft, as in the Annunciation crook, consists of two concave parts soldered together. This piece is less well preserved than the preceding one and is heavily restored in places. The gilding has disappeared almost entirely, as has the glaze of the enamel. The small beads that form the archangel's eyes are still in place; others have been lost.

Literature: Barbier de Montault, *La Bibliothèque Vaticane et ses annexes* (1867), p. 82. Stohlman, *Gli smalti del Museo Sacro Vaticano* (1939), p. 37.

*143 Inv. no. 576. Plaque with Adam Rising from the Dead.* Copper and enamel (Limoges). $8^1/_4 \times 5^3/_4$″. Early 13th century. Provenance unknown.

Adam is portrayed in the act of raising the lid of his tomb. This plaque must have been part of a story of the life of Christ after his crucifixion, entombment, and resurrection. There is general agreement that it formed a group with two plaques now in the British Museum, one with the Virgin and Saint John, the other with two angels swinging censers. The perspective is rather awkward. In fact, it is not clear whether the blue rhomboids that alternate with the green stripes represent the inside or the outside of the tomb. On the other hand, the figure of Adam is drawn with a very sure hand, even if the body lines are not always anatomically correct. The quality of the plaque is due not only to the free plastic rendering of the human figure but also to the leaf tracery *(opus vermiculatum)* engraved on the background and the bold contrasts of bright colors.

Literature: Marquet de Vasselot, "Les émaux limousins à fond vermiculé," *Revue archéologique* 6 (1905): 423. Volbach, *Itinerario*, Museo Sacro, Guida 3 (1936), p. 27. Stohlman, *Gli smalti del Museo Sacro Vaticano* (1939), pp. 31–32.

*144 Inv. no. 821. Casket for the relics of Saint Stephen.* Copper, engraved, gilded, and enameled (Limoges), over a wooden box. 6⁷/₈ (including feet) × 7 × 3¹/₈". 13th century. Provenance unknown. Mentioned in the inventory of Pope Clement XIII (1758–69).

The enamel, adorned with little circles and rosettes, provides the background against which the scene is set. The figures are in gilded metal and very accurately limned by the incised lines, which define even such details as the stones used for the saint's martyrdom. On the front of the box is depicted the scene of the stoning. The saint has sunk to his knees in fervent prayer. The slanting lid shows, on the left, the figure of Saul at whose feet one of the executioners lays his cloak; on the right, Stephen's arrest. On the gable ends (not reproduced), Saint Peter and Saint Stephen. There are no figures on the back of the box. The refined use of the enamel, whose colors set off the monochrome figures, matches the overall composition, giving the scene of the martyrdom an elegant, tranquil rhythm to the exclusion of all dramatic effect.

Literature: Barbier de Montault, *La Bibliothèque Vaticane et ses annexes* (1867), p. 82. Muñoz, *L'art byzantin à l'exposition de Grottaferrata* (1906), p. 156. Stohlman, *Gli smalti del Museo Sacro Vaticano* (1939), p. 36.

*145 Inv. no. 608. Diptych with scenes of the Passion of Christ.* Ivory. 11 × 9¹/₂ × ¹/₄". 14th century. Provenance unknown. Mentioned in the inventory of Pope Clement XIII (1758–69).

The little tablet was originally mounted on a wooden panel; the hinges have disappeared. The architectural motif (an unbroken row of pointed arches with trefoil, crockets, and flower finial, resting on extremely slender columns) divides each leaf into nine compartments. The scenes run from left to right and from the top down, many of them occupying more than one compartment. The sequence is not interrupted by the division of the leaves.

The story begins with Christ's betrayal by Judas and the payment of the thirty pieces of silver. Next comes the capture of Jesus in three compartments, one on the left-hand and two on the right-hand leaf. In the last compartment of the top row, the suicide of Judas. The second row begins with the Scourging at the Pillar, followed by the Way to Calvary (two compartments) and, on the right-hand leaf, the Crucifixion and the Deposition (which together occupy three compartments). In the bottom row, the first two compartments show the Embalming of Christ's Body; the next three the Pious Women at the Tomb; finally, the *Noli me tangere*.

The figures are elongated, their attitudes calm and collected. The small heads and the parallel folds of the drapery, the simple rhythm and the strong feeling for plastic values, justify the attribution of the work to a north Italian artist from the Venetian mainland, perhaps from Padua, who had assimilated Giottesque influences.

Beginning at the tenth compartment, the forms undergo a drastic change. The figures become less static; the drapery tends to sway and crease; more important still, the proportions are altered. This is especially noticeable in the Crucifixion, where the length of Christ's body is out of all proportion to Mary's, and still more in the Deposition, where the Virgin is head and shoulders taller than the other figures. The scenes with the Three Pious Women and the *Noli me tangere* offer clear evidence that the magnificent diptych was not carved by a single artist, though the craftsmen who took a hand in it worked under a central guidance and kept to a pre-established architectural plan. It is chiefly the architecture that warrants the conclusion that the ivory, even though carved in Italy, derives from French models.

Literature: Kanzler, *Gli avori dei Musei Profano e Sacro della Biblioteca Vaticana* (1903), II, no. 61. Morey, *Gli oggetti di avorio e di osso del Museo Sacro Vaticano* (1936), pp. 77–78.

*146 Inv. no. 70 (De' Rossi). Virgin and Child.* Ivory. 5¹/₄ × 2³/₈ (base) × 1³/₈" (base). Mid-14th century. Provenance unknown.

As far as the inconography is concerned, this ivory is one of those in which the Infant Jesus reveals a frontal conception whereas the Virgin is viewed from three-quarters. In accordance with tradition, Jesus is portrayed in the hieratical posture of benediction. His mother is treated more naturalistically, indeed anecdotically—playing with the Child and offering him a ball.

Originally the group was colered; now only the gilding on the girdle and a little of the red lining of the mantle can still be seen. It will be noticed that the Child's head shows no trace of a crown. From this it may be inferred that the Virgin too was originally uncrowned, though her head is flattened at the top.

The drapery, at once limp and firm, and the fact that the modeling is not broken even by the intersection of the various planes seem to point to an artist from the north of France. On the other hand, the overall sturdiness and in particular the almond-shaped eyes and smiling faces might warrant the attribution of the work to a Sienese artist influenced by Tino di Camaino's late period.

Literature: Kanzler, *Gli avori dei Musei Profano e Sacro della Biblioteca Vaticana* (1903), II, no. 31. Morey, *Gli oggetti di avorio e di osso del Museo Sacro Vaticano* (1936), p. 76.

*147 Inv. no. 633 a–b. Diptych with scenes from the life of Jesus and Mary.* Ivory. 12 × 7¹/₂ × ¹/₂". First half of the 14th century. Provenance unknown. Mentioned in the inventory of Pope Clement XIII (1758–69).

Each scene occupies three arches, of which the one in the middle is wider but not higher than the other two. This stresses the centrality of the composition. Very few of the slender supporting columns can be seen: the figures block them from view. The arches in the top row are surmounted by steep gables, between which rise tall slender towers very well designed architecturally.

The scenes are not arranged in chronological order. From left to right and from top to bottom: The Coronation of the Virgin, performed by an angel at Christ's command; at each side a pair of angels, one kneeling with a candlestick, the other standing in prayer behind the first. The Last Judgment, with very few figures in order to preserve the symmetry and spaciousness that characterize the entire composition. The Annunciation and the Nativity are united in one section; in the Nativity, the Infant Jesus is not represented in the crib but in his mother's arms; another unusual feature is that Saint Joseph is shown in conversation with the Virgin. In the Crucifixion, the arrangement of the figures aims at achieving eurhythmy at the cost of dramatic effect. The Massacre of the Innocents and the Flight into Egypt again occupy a single section. Next comes the Deposition, which is more agitated. But the tranquil symmetry that dominates the work returns in the last two scenes—the Adoration of the Magi and the Entombment.

Some scholars (Volbach) view the diptych as a French work of the late thirteenth century. Others (Morey) believe it is north Italian from the first half of the fourteenth.

Literature: Kanzler, *Gli avori dei Musei Profano e Sacro della Biblioteca Vaticana* (1903), II, no. 62. Morey, *Gli oggetti di avorio e di osso del Museo Sacro Vaticano* (1936), p. 76. Volbach, *Itinerario*, Museo Sacro, Guida 3 (1936), p. 18.

*148 Inv. no. 615. Diptych with scenes from the life of Jesus and the Last Judgment.* Ivory. $6^5/_8 \times 8^7/_8$". Second half of the 14th century. From the Museo Vettori. Mentioned in the inventory of Pope Clement XIII (1758–69).

This work, unlike the previous one, is divided into plain compartments without architectural motifs. The sequence of the scenes begins at the bottom and proceeds from left to right with the Annunciation followed by the Nativity (in an unusually rich environment: an artfully draped curtain hangs in the upper foreground). Next come the Adoration of the Magi, the Presentation in the Temple, the Crucifixion, the Entombment, the Resurrection, and the *Noli me tangere*. The top row differs from the other two in the close crowding of the figures. The representation of the Resurrection is peculiar in that all we can see of Christ is his feet. Next comes the Descent of the Holy Ghost and, on the right-hand leaf, the Holy Trinity in an unusual iconographic treatment: God the Father is enclosed in a lozenge with the Dove issuing from his mouth, while Christ is represented as a child instead of as crucified. In the corners, the emblems of the four Evangelists. The series ends with the Last Judgment.

Volbach recognizes in this work the impact of French cathedral sculpture. In Morey's opinion, it was executed by a German artist under French influence.

Literature: Gori, *Thesaurus veterum dipticorum* (1759), 3: 290. Morey, *Gli oggetti di avorio e di osso del Museo Sacro Vaticano* (1936), p. 82. Volbach, *Avori Medioevali*, Museo Sacro, Guida 5 (1942), p. 14.

*149 Inv. no. 5006 (left), 5008 (right), 5007 (below). Three mirror backs.* Ivory. Diameters $3^1/_8$" (left); $2^7/_8$" (right); $3^7/_8$" (below). 14th and 15th century. Provenance unknown.

All three pieces are decorated with secular scenes. The first shows two chess players in a room adorned with curtains. The second, which is edged with floral motifs, represents a courting scene with a falconer and a lady who is restraining an unruly cat; the encounter is set in the shade of a tree at whose foot a spring gushes from an antique mask. The third mirror back also shows a courting scene: a youth kneels before a lady who is holding a crown and sketching a dance step. The arches that frame the scene contain naturalistic motifs (flowers and foliage); the grotesque masks in the spandrels derive undoubtedly from French *drôleries*. The whole work shows traces of gilding and color; the background still has the original deep blue.

The unconstrained conception and working out of the scenes, the bold modeling of the figures based on a well-knit design, the anecdotic presentation, and particularly the skillful adaptation of the composition to the circular shape prove that all three pieces have a French origin. They probably date from the early fifteenth century. The second and third may be by the same hand or at least from the same workshop.

Literature: Volbach, *Avori Medioevali*, Museo Sacro, Guida 5 (1942), p. 14.